IMPROVE YOUR PE

WHAT OTHERS WANT TO HEAR

How To Talk To Anyone With Confidence and Charisma Through Effective Communication Skills

Jayden Navarro

Table of Contents

PART I 8
Chapter 1: Different Emotions and How to Handle Them 21
Chapter 2: Meditation for Emotion 30
Chapter 3: Self-Discipline 39
What it Takes to Develop Self-Discipline 41
Keeping Yourself Accountable 41
Having Rewards and Penalties 42
Make a Commitment 43
Chapter 1: Learning About Memory 45
Chapter 2: Thinking and Problem Solving 55
Chapter 3: Learning and Attention Performance 63
CHAPTER ONE 78
CHAPTER TWO 82
A Loop 83
Problems 84
CHAPTER THREE 85
Eating Habits 86
Smoking Habits 87
Drinking Habits 89
Using your Triggers 90
CHAPTER FOUR 91
A Big Break 93
Classical Conditioning 98
Procrastination 100
Be Prepared 101
CHAPTER FIVE 103
CHAPTER SIX 111
The Three R's 112
Step by Step 114
Switch Bad for Good 116
CHAPTER SEVEN 119
CHAPTER EIGHT 123
Use it or lose it 124
CHAPTER NINE 133
Simple meditation practice 137
FINALE 281

PART I

8

Introduction

It was not a long time ago that I was struggling with social anxiety. Talking with other people made me very uncomfortable and scared. At first, I thought that I was just shy—or at least this what my parents told me growing up. Being known as the "shy kid" gave me an excuse to avoid facing my fears and problems. However, it came to a point where I decided to change for the better. I had enough of always shaking when ordering a drink at a club or purchasing a newspaper. I knew I could change and I wanted to do it.

This is the reason why I decided to start researching about social skills and how to apply them in the everyday life. I spent hours and hours over books and videos, trying to grasp the secret of those who were having a successful social life.

The following chapters will discuss the primary preparedness principals that you will need to apply if you ever hope to really be ready to face a social situation without any issue. Before getting started and diving into the topic, here are a few things to consider and keep in mind. One of the things that will make the biggest difference is the amount of time you spend practicing. As with any other skill, being able to socialize properly takes time with a lot of trial and error. Do not underestimate this part. The last thing before getting started is the ability to try to make a small change every single day. Every day is a new opportunity to build a bit more self-confidence and become better at the social game, so be sure practice on a daily basis.

There are plenty of books on this subject on the market. Thanks again for choosing this one! Every effort was made to ensure it is full of as much useful information as possible. Please enjoy!

Chapter 1: We are social animals

As Aristotle said, humans are social animals. This was the first notion that I came across when I started my journey to become a better social player and increase my social skills. However, one question kept arising in my head. If we are truly social animals, why is it so hard for so many people to convey their message without turning red or start shaking? I decided that "shyness" was not a satisfying answer and started digging deeper. I found out that, over time, several factors may justify a difficulty in this area. Here are the most common ones:

1. Inadequate learning of social skills can be determined by the impossibility of observing adults who surround us—sufficiently effectively and protracted over time—or who surrounds us and shapes our education also has difficulty confronting social situations. As a result, the skills that are necessary cannot be acquired. Why? Because we learn by emulating others and if there is a lack of practical examples, there is no way we are able to get social practices in our system.

2. There is a lack of positive reinforcement from the surrounding environment. This can be linked to the lack of both valid social contacts and positive feedback that are necessary for the development and consolidation of social skills.

3. A symptom characterized by social anxiety that can reach an intensity that prevents the subject from using all or part of his abilities. This is why having social troubles does not correspond

with being ignorant or not having anything to say. The content is there; it is just difficult to pull it out.

4. The presence of side effects of drugs that can make it difficult to approach social situations. In fact, even if most people think that alcohol can help them become better social players, it is a game that does not last for a very long time. In fact, even if it is true that drinking makes anyone more sociable, it is also true that after the effect has gone away, the insecurity begins to increase. I strongly recommend staying away from alcohol and drugs, especially when working on social skills.

At this point, I was wondering: what can I do to improve my social skills? I knew that there was a way. I just had not found it yet. Then something changed.

I started taking courses on how to date women and know more people. Day after day, month after month, I began to see tangible progress and, soon enough, I became a strong social player. In the next chapters, I will discuss the main strategies I have applied to transform who I was.

Chapter 2: What are social skills?

Social skills are those skills that we use every day in life to communicate and interact with other people, both individually and in groups.

People with strong social skills are usually more successful in both professional and personal life because they move well in a team and are able to communicate effectively with other people. Having suffered from social anxiety, I know that hurts, but it is just the truth.

A person (or a leader) who is good at these skills is basically a great communicator.

Social skills are the culmination of other dimensions of emotional intelligence. Social skills move people to go in the direction they want, with the strong awareness that nothing important is done alone, but teamwork and community effort is fundamental.

What I discovered is that social skills can be divided into two groups:

1. the skills that influence people, such as influence, communication, conflict management, inspiration, and change;

2. the skills that generate collaboration, such as knowing how to build bonds, collaboration, and knowing how to work in a team.

It's never too late to improve your social skills (I started at the age of 40). The first step is to honestly examine yourself and admit that you need to improve in your deficient areas.

Let's find out some tips that will help you do it.

Chapter 3: Nine Strategies to Improve your social skills

During my researches, I discovered that there were essentially nine strategies that successful people applied to be a great social player. I started practicing them all, one after the other. I strongly believe that anyone can become a good social actor, but only with the right guidance. Even if at the beginning it might be a struggle, when you start seeing your life to change in every aspect, a strong motivation will kick in and drag you forward. In fact, I discovered that there is a relevant correspondence between the ability to socialize and success in other aspects of life. For instance, good social skills make it simpler to influence people and make new friends, craft powerful and long-lasting relationship, and climb the corporate ladder.

If you feel or know that you are not a very social person, it is fundamental to study how to build this aspect of your character. Here are the nine strategies that will help you get started on your journey.

1. Learn how to Listen

People are often centered on themselves, and because of this, many are used to not allow the other person to have their turn to speak. This can result in a frustrating situation, where the other interlocutor perceives you as rude.

I, too, often did it and maybe I will do it again in the future. But once I started to try to focus my mind on the other person by forgetting about myself, being able to feel better what other people say or want to say, everything started to change for the better. Suddenly, I was able to offer better advice, enjoy the conversation much more, and build stronger relationships. One trick that I used was to look at the mouth of the other person. In this way, I was focusing all my energy to the point where their voice was coming from. This allowed me to exclude any distraction and get more inside their point of view. It is a great social practice and I recommend you to try it out.

2. Be really *interested in other people*

If you start paying more attention towards other people, you will be naturally perceived as a better individual. Furthermore, this will allow you to become a better listener as well since you will get deeper into other people's feelings and points of view.

Only by opening your heart and truly listening to what other individuals want to tell you will you discover that everyone has something interesting to say. We often get too picky in what we like to talk about and that we totally exclude certain topics from our daily conversations. However, by confronting them, you will improve your social skills for sure.

When I first stumbled upon this tactic, I did not understand it fully. In fact, most people are interested in others in a fake way, which does not lead very far. Only by truly caring about other people will you be able to become a better listener. Of course, you cannot care about everyone in the same manner, so start by meeting people with the same interests you have: it will make the practice much easier.

3. Treat others how you would like to be treated

The law of reciprocity is a paradigmatic expression of how the world works. In fact, the way you treat someone else is the way he will be obliged to treat you. Karma may take some time to kick in, but rest assured that you will be rewarded for your kind actions. Furthermore, being kind has an amazing social impact on other people.

"Being one" is one of the most important aspects when it comes to social skills. Only by being aligned in everything you do will you become a better social player.

4. Keep a positive attitude

Having a positive attitude is a decision, not a coincidence. In fact, you may have noticed that there are people who are always calm and cool, while others tend to get caught up in situations. You may not be able to do it all the time, but keeping a positive attitude is something that can be learned and "installed" in your mental system. Everyone likes positive people, so do not overlook this important social treat. When a problem arises, before focusing on the bad side, and with proper exercise, you will begin to see opportunities and what's good in any person or situation.

Obviously, this does not mean you should avoid difficult conversations or skip through issues when other people bring them up. However, you can influence the course of the discussion by sharing positive points of view and helping others to not give up. By doing so, you will become "the positive guy," which is a great social role to play.

5. Be silent and speak less

At first, when I was trying to improve my social skills, I thought that, in order to practice, I had to talk all the time. However, I discovered that there are certain interesting advantages in being a much quieter person. First of all, being silent is a great way to work on your listening skills and avoid unnecessary fights, reducing the possibility of a falling out that may arise from you criticizing them (even if you do not mean to). Especially if you are facing a topic that you do not know too much about, let the other person carry on the conversation and just go with the flow, adding appropriate and valuable comments from time to time.

6. Communicate more than with your words

To become a better communicator you have to improve the way you say something, filling up your words with physical excitement and tangible passion.

Your attitude, as previously stated, can physically modify your body, making you look more open or close, depending on your emotions. For example, if you are feeling calm, open, and relaxed, this will be expressed by your body and vice versa. When you listen, for example, you can keep a passionate eye contact with the other interlocutor to transmit the sensation that you are actually listening to him.

Learning and understanding body language is a great tool in your arsenal and something that I highly encourage you to develop.

7. Break the ice effectively.

When you first meet a new person, I suggest you begin with a generic topic, rather than a personal one. You can talk about current events, comment on the weather, a compliment, or an observation. To chat is not always easy. In fact, it can happen to go into the ball and not know what to say. Here are some practical ideas that have helped me in many situations:

- "I like your hat. Where did you buy it?"

- "The climate is really crazy. What do you think is going on?"

- "I like a lot the view from here! What do you think about it?"

- "These lessons are really interesting, don't you think?"

8. Find ways to prolong the conversation.

After breaking the ice with general topics such as current events or the weather, try to go a bit more on the personal side of things. Ask questions about family, work or personal ideas can stimulate and deepen a dialogue. Remember that you need at least two people to talk, so do not talk too much or too little. Ask open-ended questions, such as those beginning with "Come," "Why," and "What," rather than a closed answer. Here are some ideas to stimulate conversation progress:

- "So, what's your job?"

- "Tell me a little bit more about your family."

- "How did you meet the landlord?"

- "How long have you been going to this place / Do you practice this activity?"

- "Do you have any plans for the bridge?"

By asking questions you let the other people "do the job" and you can practice active listening (remember strategy number one?).

9. Avoid delicate subjects with strangers

At first, I thought that by bringing up "heavy topics" I would be seen as the intelligent guy. However, I heard on my behalf that when you break the ice with someone you do not know well, you should avoid certain issues such as disputes over religion, politics, race, and sexual orientation. For example:

- You can ask a general question about the elections, but it is often considered inappropriate to ask someone who they will vote for.

- You can ask generic questions about a person's religious faith, but there is no need to deepen the ideas that a religion has on matters such as sex.

These are the nine strategies that have allowed me to work on my social skills and become a better communicator. As I have told already, practice is the secret. Get yourself in social situations and start applying them. You will be amazed by the quick progress you will be able to make.

PART II

Chapter 1: Different Emotions and How to Handle Them

There are many different emotions that a person experiences and each one of these emotions can have a range of facets that make what each person feels a wholly unique experience. This means that what you experience when you meet a new person will be entirely different from the experience you would get from anyone else. Every person is a different feeling when you first meet them, and this is a great way to learn to distinguish whose feelings you are feeling, even when you cannot experience them.

However, to be able to distinguish a person from the emotional identification card they leave, you must first be able to first understand the different emotions and be able to distinguish them from the other emotions in the atmosphere. You also have to learn how to harness them for yourself, and really get in tune with them Then, eventually, you will be able to identify someone by the emotions they leave behind. This chapter will inform you of the different emotions, and how you can understand them better.

Happiness

Happiness is a common emotion for people to experience, however, it has many different factors in it. There are several layers of happiness, and you have to be able to discern each one from the next. Being able to do this is one of the most difficult things an emotional master does because happiness is one of the most complex emotion a person feels.

Think of the best thing in your life. How it made you feel. Now think of the day you got some good news. The happiness you experienced in those two events was probably exponentially different. This is how happiness works. You can be mildly happy, or you can be happy while sad at the same time, or you can be extremely happy. There are so many different types of happiness that it can make your head spin. For this book, we will focus on the main types of happiness, so as not to cause information overload. Here are the main types of happiness.

Joy

This is the emotion that many people experience when they hear good news. It is the emotion you experience when you find out someone you know is going to have a baby. It is the basis for all happy moments. Joy is the emotion you feel when you wake up on a Saturday morning and realize that you do not have to go to work that day, and can sleep in an extra hour. Joy is the emotion you feel when you find out that you have a little more money in the bank than you originally thought.

This is the most common happiness that people feel. It can be strong, or it can be mild. It can hit all at once, or it can build gradually. Joy is everywhere around you. People often mistake joy for other emotions of happiness, however, believing that they are synonymous. They might be in the English language, but they are not synonymous in the emotional IQ culture. Each emotion is separate, not all considered one. Joy is the basic emotion of happiness, but it is not the only one.

Elation

Elation is another facet of the emotion of happiness. Elation is what you experience when you find out you got the job promotion that you have been wanting for so long. Elation is the emotion that people who have been waiting years to conceive experience when they find out that they are expecting a baby. Elation is the purest level of happiness. It leaves the person experiencing it feeling like they are on cloud nine, and like they have never felt anything better. This is the emotion of happiness that everyone seeks out and wants to experience on a regular basis.

Most people experience elation the best when they have been through a period of sadness. The sadness allows them to truly appreciate the happiness that has been bestowed upon them. When people feel truly elated, it is because something that they have wanted to happen for a long time finally happened after a long period of struggling.

Excitement

Most people know what excitement is. It is the emotion you experience when you are wanting something, and you know that it is coming, and you are so happy that you cannot wait for it to be here. Like a kid on Christmas, or an expectant mother, to someone waiting for a package in the mail. You cannot beat the feeling of excitement. It is the most contagious of emotions that are out there. When someone sees that another person is excited, they get excited for them, just so they can feel excited too.

Most people want to feel excited about each day as they wake up, however, this is nearly impossible to achieve. They can, however, achieve the next emotion of happiness that is on our list.

General Contentment

This is the last emotion of happiness that is on the list. This is what most people strive for in their life. While most people want to experience excitement every day, they are generally willing to settle for general contentment. That is because general contentment is a great feeling to have. It is when you wake up every day thinking that it is going to be a good day, and you are generally pleased with the day's occurrences. People who experience ge happier people, and they are the ones you see great.

There are a lot of people that try to fake general contentment when in reality they are not happy at all. However, since you are reading this book, you can probably already spot those people from a mile away. The people with true general contentment are the ones that you can feel the calm rolling off of them. They are the roll with the punches kind of people that you see that never have a bad thing to say about the day no matter what day you see them. Even on Mondays.

Those are the main facets of the emotion happiness. There are more subtle ones, but you could write an entire book on all the subtle nuances of happiness, and for a beginner, that is a lot of information to process in one sitting. These ones are the ones that you will experience most in the beginning. However, there are many places that you can research online to learn more about this emotion when you are ready.

Sadness

Sadness is an emotion a lot of people face. It is pretty complex as well, just like with happiness. However, it does not have as many facets, just different levels of sadness. These levels do not really have

, and they are hard to identify as anything other than sadness. The difference is when someone is depressed, as opposed to sad. With depression, not only is the sadness overwhelming, the complete apathy for everything that rolls off of them is scary. Yet, when you look at the faces of these people, they seem like the happiest people on earth.

Sadness is not depression, though. Sadness is just an emotion that you experience when something that is upsetting happens. You can experience sadness when you do not get something right, or do not get what you want. These are a few of the more general types of sadness. The slightly dark feeling you get when you are upset.

Sadness can also raise in intensity. The feeling of sadness you get after a bad break up, for example. The cliché is that the woman sits on her couch watching chick flicks while eating ice cream straight from the tub, and the guy goes out to the bar to drink away the pain. However, many people cope with sadness differently. Some may stay in bed until they feel better, some may go for a run to make themselves feel better.

Sadness can increase in intensity even more than the pain you feel during a breakup. The sadness you feel when tragedy strikes. Such as losing a loved one or a pet. This sadness can easily turn into depression if not addressed soon enough. This level of sadness often feels like a hole has been ripped in your chest. Like you could never breathe again. This is the worst type of sadness, and the hardest to get through, but if someone can get through it, they may be able to escape the grasp of depression.

Anger

Anger is one of the least complex emotions you will experience. It is pretty straightforward. However, it is also the hardest emotion to describe. Anger is like a searing branding iron is trying to rip its way out of your soul through your stomach. It leaves you feeling like you want to scream, or punch someone, or curse up a storm. I think the reason that anger is so hard to explain is that everyone experienced it so differently. It may not be very complex in that it doesn't have a lot of levels or facets, but it is experienced differently by person to person. More so than any other emotion out there. Anger can cause a wash of sadness over some people. Some people when they are angry feel strangely happy. Some people respond with mild anger on intense things, but rage on little things. It is all dependent on the person themselves, and that is why anger can be one of the hardest things to explain.

Anger can be found in many places. Most of the time it is when someone is mean to another person, however, some people respond to sad things with anger. Anger is often used as a synonym for frustration, but this is not the case. Far from it, actually. Frustration is just mild irritation at a slight annoyance. Anger is the feeling of great agitation at things that are considered harmful or offensive.

Jealousy

This is an emotion that everyone will experience in their lifetime, but no one will want to admit it. That is because, in a lot of religions, it is considered a sin. This one is one of the most hidden emotions, but one of the easiest to feel once you are tuned into it. Jealousy is the emotion that people experience when they want something that someone else has. Jealousy is also used to describe how a woman or man feels in a relationship. Do not confuse this, as it is not truly jealousy. Jealousy is when you want something that is not yours. When you already have something, and you want to protect it, that is being territorial.

Jealousy is often felt with a sick feeling in the stomach and is portrayed as a puke green aura. Have you ever heard the phrases "green with envy" or "sick with jealousy"? These are because that is the energy that this emotion gives off, and can really affect an emotional master because it is a strong emotion, due to the fact that it is generally buried deep beneath the surface, and it builds pressure until it is to the point where if it were a gas, it would cause the person feeling this emotion to literally explode.

Those are the different emotions that people experience on a regular, or semi-regular basis. Now that you know them, and their basic identifiers, you can move on to how to harness their usage to handle a situation.

Chapter 2: Meditation for Emotion

There are many ways to unlock your emotional IQ and really access it, but meditation is the best way to do so. It allows you to center yourself enough to make sure that you are finding the right part of yourself to unlock. A lot of times even if you do not do it right, you can trick yourself into thinking that you have, and you will feel like you are seeing the world when really it is a placebo effect and you are just as blind as you were before. So meditation is a great choice, though other choices will be discussed in a later chapter just to cover all options.

What is Meditation?

Meditation is the act of calming yourself and slowing your breathing to truly find your center. It is used by people from all walks of life, though it is mainly attributed to being used by monks to find inner peace. However, anyone can meditate and find it effective. You do not have to be an expert either. There are so many tutorials out there. This chapter will cover meditation techniques as well, to ensure that you are learning everything you need to know about opening your emotional IQ. You want to open it to find yourself, and meditation will help with that.

Meditation involves being able to sit still for long periods of time, so it can be difficult at first. Even more so if you are someone who is always moving, and never slows down. Because you have to slow down for meditation to even work. When you are meditating, you are literally putting yourself into a trance, and your heart will slow to the pace that it functions at when you are asleep.

Meditation is used to find spirituality, along with a whole list of other things, including the emotional IQ. Here is a list of things that meditation helps with.

☐ Anxiety: Anxiety is a problem that plagues a lot of people. It causes raised heart rate, intense and sometimes borderline asthmatic breathing problems, and thoughts that can be suicidal, or homicidal. Anxiety attacks can leave the person who suffers from them emotionally and physically exhausted. Anxiety is also something that can be almost entirely cured my meditation

☐

The reason for that is when you meditate you calm yourself enough to figure out what is causing your anxiety so you can address and fix the problem. You want to be able to do that when it comes to your inner eye so that your vision is not clouded by your fears and panic attacks.

☐ Stress: Stress can cause a lot of problems in your life. It is the number one cause of heart attacks due to the fact that it can raise your blood pressure. It can also cause strokes and other health issues. You do not want to die due to stress as it is not a pleasant way to go.

Meditation helps you slow your heart rate and work through the things that are bothering you to ensure that you are living a healthy lifestyle. You want to be healthy, otherwise, you will find that your life will not be as enjoyable as you would hope. You want to enjoy your life. Stress can also cloud your emotional IQ just as anxiety does, and it can cause anxiety as well. You want to have a freed up emotional IQ so that you can find yourself.

☐ Ease Pain: By slowing your heart and breath rate, you are dulling the nerve endings in your body, allowing the pain receptors to have a break. This helps you recover from severe pain, and end chronic pain. Pain can affect your everyday life in ways that some people can never imagine. It leaves you tired, drained, and wondering where you are going to get the energy to even eat.

You do not want to live with chronic pain, but unfortunately, some people have no choice. If you meditate, however, you will be able to ease your pain for a while in order to get your energy back so that you can take on the world. This is a good thing because pain can cloud your mind, not just your emotional IQ, but your entire mind.

☐ Calm Your Soul: This is a good thing that you can use meditation for. If anything is bothering you, you can use meditation to really figure out what exactly is nagging at the back of your mind. You want to have a clear head when you go to use your emotional IQ, otherwise, you will find that what is bothering you will make its way into your sight and cause you to have some issues deciphering what is real and what is fabricated by your emotions.

It is important to separate your emotions from your emotional IQ because you have to stay completely neutral on any topic you are looking for clarity on. Otherwise, your "vision" may be skewed in the direction of your worry. You do not want that to happen, as it can cause unnecessary stress, which as mentioned above is bad for your health.

☐ Stabilize Your Life: It is important to stabilize your life because maintaining balance is essential to succeed in your life. If you do not have balance, you will have problems keeping an organized life. Having a clear and stable life is good for your health as well because you are more likely to make healthier choices. This will extend your life and make it easier to access your emotional IQ. It is proven that the healthier you are, the easier it is to clear your mind.

There are many other things that meditation can do for some people that it cannot do for others. It is best to try it for yourself to see if it works for you. Of course, if you do not know how to meditate, it can make it harder to do so, so let us go over how to meditate successfully.

How to Meditate

There are many different ways to meditate, but meditation is important to do correctly, otherwise, you will find yourself not getting the full benefits of the process, as you would if you do it correctly. So for a beginner, it is best to not take any shortcuts and to really go the full nine yards to do it correctly.

It will take some time to really learn how to clear your mind, so if you do not get it on the first try, do not get discouraged. No one gets it on the first try, and that can get frustrating, but it is completely normal. You want to keep trying to clear your mind. If you get discouraged after the first try, you won't be able to truly know if you can do it or not. Media portrays meditation as something you can do with ease and something that everyone is able to just sit and do, but it is not. It takes a lot of self-restraint. So let's go over the steps.

☐ Step One: The first step is to find a quiet place where you will not be interrupted. Even if it means going into the bathroom and turning the shower on to find some peace and quiet. You have to be quiet and undisturbed in order to find your inner peace. If you are not in a peaceful area, finding your center will be extremely hard because there will be so many distractions in the area that you will not be able to concentrate on yourself.

☐

☐ Step Two: Sit in a comfortable position. A lot of people choose the crossed leg style because that is what they know, but if it is not a comfortable position for you, then you will not be able to focus on yourself because you will be too distracted by your leg going numb, your back hurting, your hips getting stiff. If you cannot focus on anything other than your discomfort, then you are not going to be able to successfully meditate. So find the most comfortable sitting position for you, even if it means in a chair. However, do not lay down. It is too easy to fall asleep if you are laying down, because your body equates the slow heartbeat and breathing with sleep, and your brain will begin to slow as well. You want the health benefits of sleeping with the full mental capabilities of being awake. Otherwise, you will not be able to probe your mind the way you would when sitting. How you sit does not matter, as long as you are comfortable.

☐

☐ Step Three: Focus on your breathing. Most people say to focus on your heart rate at first, but that is a lot harder, and if you slow your breathing, generally your heart will follow suit. You want to really focus on your breath though. Do not let yourself get distracted. Breathe in for four counts and out for four counts. Balance is key. In fact, why don't you give it a try right now? You don't have to try to meditate, just work on the breathing.

Sit comfortably, and close your eyes. Breathe in for four counts through your nose. Hold it for two counts, and then let it out of your mouth for four seconds. Focus on keeping a steady rhythm. If you lose count, then start again. You have to make sure that you are keeping the rhythm and not losing count, otherwise, you will not be able to focus on the meditation if you can't keep your breathing steady. Try doing a repetition of ten, and once you get that down, try upping it to twenty, and so on and so forth. The longer you can go while focusing on your breathing, the easier it will be to transition your focus to your mental state once you get to that point.

☐ Step Four: Ignore the twinges. This is something that is one of the hardest things to do when you are trying to get into meditation because our bodies are not meant to sit still for extended periods of time. After five to ten minutes of sitting still, you will begin to feel itchy in places such as your nose or your head. Maybe your leg will start to feel like it is going to fall asleep. Ignore all of these. They are signals from your brain to your body checking to see if you are asleep yet or not. Once the brain realizes that the body is not responding, then it will command the body to shut down all processes as if you were asleep. If you are still awake, you will get all of the benefits of being asleep, while still getting to enjoy the benefits of being awake in a calm, unfazed perception.

☐

☐ Step Five: Once you get into this phase of pretty much lucid dreaming, slowly transition your focus from your breathing to your mind. Do this by only focusing on every other count and when you are not focusing on your count, then focus on a thought that has been on your mind all day. Eventually, you can switch your focus entirely to that thought. Once you are ready to move on you can think of other thoughts slowly until you are fully immersed in your own mind.

☐

☐ Step Six: Explore your mind freely. Get to know every little nook and cranny of your brain. This step will take some time to get to, as you will need to be able to hold the meditation stage for quite a while before you can freely explore your mind. However, once you get to this stage, you will be able to learn more about yourself than you probably ever wanted to know. This is important because you want to know everything about yourself. This includes the good, bad, and even the ugly. The more you know, the more clear your vision can be.

☐

☐ Step Seven: This is the final step of meditation, known as the outro. A lot of people think that you can just snap out of a meditation, and some people can, although it is not very healthy for you because the sudden return of a normal heart rate stresses your heart out, and it can cause some severe headaches as well. You have to gradually enter yourself back into reality. If you do not, you will have a problem with being confused, headaches, and much more. To come back to reality without these problems, simply revert your focus slowly back onto your breathing, and focus on speeding up your breathing until your heart rate returns to normal.

Once you have successfully managed to meditate for the first time, you will find that every time after that you can begin to get a little faster with your meditation. This is a good thing because when you meditate, sometimes you do not have a lot of time, however, you still have to ease out of it. So it is good to be able to get quick at it in order to have ample time to ease out of it.

Remember, the first several times it can be extremely difficult for you to get into a trance state if you even manage to at all. Do not get discouraged if you cannot do it immediately. Also, even if you do get into a trance state it may be hard for you to maintain it for any length of time. This is normal and is nothing to feel bad about. Keep trying, and eventually, you will be able to meditate like a Tibetan Monk.

Chapter 3: Self-Discipline

It is important for you to have self-discipline when you want to improve your emotional IQ. It will help you harness your emotions exponentially so that you can work on keeping them under control. Here is how you can do that.

About Improving Self Discipline

You are probably aware that self-discipline is a great trait to have, and maybe you are not as disciplined as you should be. If that is the case, you may find it hard to keep your mind and emotions in check. If you are not able to control your emotions, your emotional IQ will be way below what it should be.

To truly understand self-discipline, you must first know the definition of what it is.

Self-discipline is defined as the ability to find a reason to stick with something for a long period of time, even if you may not want to. Especially if you do not want to.

This may seem confusing because it doesn't seem possible to find a reason to do something when you obviously do not want to do it. However, the truth is that there are reasons you may never have even known about to do what you do not want to do. Most of those come from inside yourself. The biggest reason should be for your emotional health. The more it wears down, the less you understand your own emotions.

Why You Should Improve

Do you have days where you just feel worn out? Maybe not even just physically, but mentally and emotionally as well? Do those days seem to be more often than not? If this is the case, you need to work on handling your emotions with more strength and understanding.

The reason you feel so drained is that you are letting yourself get too emotionally worked up by little things. It is human nature to get upset easily it seems. However, with a little effort in the discipline area, you can increase your emotional strength and intelligence quite a bit. This will help you find the strength to ignore the irritating things and live a happier life.

What it Takes to Develop Self-Discipline

No one is born with innate amounts of self-discipline. We are all born with a need to take care of, rather than a need to take care of others. That is why babies are not born able to walk. You have to develop yourself discipline beyond what you may naturally develop growing up.

Most people need a few things to happen to be able to work on their self-discipline, and that is okay because developing self-discipline in itself takes a form of discipline that not everyone is used to.

You have to know how to build your self-discipline though, as it does not happen overnight. You should also remember that you have taken years to be who you are, and you should not expect to change completely in a short amount of time. You have to give yourself the time to really become a better, more disciplined person. One of the hardest things about having self-discipline is developing it, and a lot of people give up before they hit their goal. So always remember to never give up, and to follow these tips to help you out.

Keeping Yourself Accountable

You are responsible for your own emotions. You cannot hold someone else responsible for how you feel, even if they make you feel that way. You can ask them to apologize for upsetting you, but in the end, it is up to you to feel better. Wallowing in your self-pity, and holding a grudge shows a low emotional IQ, and is what you want to work to stay away from. At the end of the day, you should be able to let go of everything that is bothering you and set yourself free from the chains of negativity.

Having Rewards and Penalties

Just like when you were a child, you should reward yourself for the good, and penalize yourself for the bad. Remember, you have to hold yourself accountable, and this means to only reward yourself for a good job. If you go a day without letting negativity bother you, or getting emotionally overstimulated from a minor transgression, buy yourself an ice cream cone. If you did happen to let your emotions control you, you don't get the ice cream cone. Of course the reward doesn't have to be ice cream, that is merely an example of how you should handle the situations.

The reason you should have a rewards system is that it helps you hold yourself accountable. If you had no rewards coming for a job well done, would you be just as eager to do the job right? Most people would not. It helps give you a reason to get better and to discipline yourself.

Rewarding yourself for a job well done also helps you see how far you have come based on a number of times you have been able to reward yourself. This will keep you from being discouraged, and feel like you are making no progress. Remember, staying on the track to being self-disciplined is a discipline all on its own.

Make a Commitment

You have to be committed to your goal if you want to get yourself where you want to go. You can't just make a goal with the attitude "If I don't get there, oh well.". You have to make a goal with an "I will do whatever it takes to make that goal" attitude. This is how you go from just a person with a goal, to a person who is going to make a change.

When you make a commitment to be stronger with your emotions, you are making a commitment to having a happier, healthier life. If you want to feel free from emotional chains you have to be more self-disciplined, and not let anyone control your emotions, or let your emotions control you. You have to make a commitment to being in control of your emotions. Without that commitment, you are likely to fall back into your old ways. No one wants to see you fail, and you should not want to see yourself fail. When you make that commitment, make it with every fiber of your being.

It doesn't matter if you tell the world about your goal, or if you keep it to yourself. All that matters is that you make that goal, and you commit to following through with every aspect that will get you to that goal.

PART III

Chapter 1: Learning About Memory

The best way to improve your memory is to understand how it works.

Memory is the space in the mind where information is stored, and used from there. It can be encoded and decoded all from the one area of the brain that controls it.

Imagine that memory is a library of all the information that you have ever encountered in your life. Libraries often have rotating books. Your memory as well has rotating information. Just like libraries, the information that is rotated is based on the importance of said information.

For example, if you are not going to see a person ever again, you will only need to know their name for the duration of the conversation you are having with them, and then you don't need to remember it any further. This would use your short term memory. However, if you work with someone every day, you would need to know their name for a long amount of time. Therefore, you would commit their name to your long-term memory.

There are two forms of memory. The first form, which is called declarative, is where you physically commit something to memory. If you see something that you deem is important, you make yourself remember. Example, repeating a phone number in your head several times until you remember it.

Then there is a non-declarative memory. This is the memory you have no recollection of trying to remember. There are some things that your brain subconsciously remembers, such as street names as you pass by them.

Memory can be sometimes faulty. It is not perfect. There are lots of factors and variables that affect your memory such as the attention you provide to your different stimulus when trying to remember something and the amount of important you see on something.

Your long-term memory may fade over time if a memory has not been called upon in a while. Just as an old photograph fades, so do memories. You may find you forget how a loved one's voice sounds when they have been gone for a long time, for example.

Sensory memory

Sensory memory is a memory that is tied to your senses. Pretty much self-explanatory. However, there is more to it than that. This memory is often only committed to short term memory.

There are three types of sensory memories. There are the memories from sight, hearing, and haptic, which has to deal with touch and taste, and smell. Scientists do not know why touch, smell, and taste use the same memory functions, but they do. Hearing seems to be the most rapidly decaying in memory, while haptic seems to commit almost instantly to long term memory.

Short-term memory

Can be used alongside the term working memory. This is your memory that remembers something for a short amount of time, and then forgets it. The memories that are forgotten are often quickly are ones that are not important. Such as things you pass in a store, or someone you see on the street.

Short term memory seems to react the most to auditory stimuli. This means that when you hear something, it can be harder to forget it than when you see it.

Long-term memory

Long term memory is where you remember things for an indefinite period of time. It can decay over time. However, some things may stick with a person forever. It seems like haptic memories stay with a person the longest, even after hearing and sight memories have faded.

Long-term memory is recorded episodically and semantically, unlike the auditory fashion in which the short-term memory is recorded. This means that people may have a hard time remembering sounds over time, but they can remember things they have seen, and patterns they have noticed. Long-term memory is a bit of a mystery even to this day on how it works exactly because everyone remembers things differently.

The type of memory most people work on is their long term memory. This takes a lot of work to build up because you really cannot fight DNA. However, you can delay the onset of memory issues by strengthening your memory.

Diet

The first thing that you should work on is your diet. If you have a poor diet, then you are going to have too much fat stored in your body. Your memory relies on your body burning rather than storing fat. This is because the ketones that are created when you burn fat are essential for the creation of memory. Ketones are pretty much brain food.

To keep ketones burning, you should try the ketogenic diet. This is where you eat fewer carbs and more fat and protein to put your body in a state of ketosis. Ketosis is where you are constantly burning ketones in your body. The ketogenic diet also helps fight Alzheimer Disease. Here is some more information about the keto diet.

4. **What is it?**

The Ketogenic diet, which is often shortened to just being called the keto diet, is a diet that is very high in fat, and low in carbs. It is proven to be a successful diet and is linked to helping prevent or even subside several health conditions, such as diabetes, epilepsy, and even Alzheimer's. This diet is used all around the world and will change what you thought you knew about carbs and fats.

This diet is obtained by drastically reducing one's carb intake. You replace the carbs that you would have eaten with fats, which makes your body focus on burning the fats that you are consuming and moving on the fats in your body. This process is known as ketosis, which puts the body into a constant fat burning state. It also burns ketones in your liver. This is how this diet combats Alzheimer's. Ketones increase brain function, and supply healthier blood to the brain, to keep the person sharp as a tack, and ready to remember, and think, about anything.

This diet also reduces blood sugar and insulin levels, so it is great if you have diabetes, or are pre-diabetic. By following this diet, if you have type two diabetes, you could actually reduce the effects of your condition, and get it under control, to the point where you may not need your medicine as often.

This diet started out in the medicinal world in the nineteen twenties. It has been around for a long time but was only recently brought to public light. It started out as an effective treatment for people with epilepsy. That's right, it began as a diet to help ease the problems from seizures, and help people control their lives. It was kind of overshadowed for a while, however, as other technologies came into play, and new medicines were introduced, but once it was determined that the medicine did not help over thirty percent of patients, the diet was reintroduced into the medical field, and brought back into popularity in helping epileptic people gain some semblance of normalcy back into their lives.

5. How Does It Work?

Your body needs calories to run. There are three types of calories. The calories that you get from protein, carbs, and fat. You want to make sure that you are getting most of your calories from fat. However, not just any fat. You want to get your calories from unsaturated fats, as these are the ones that burn ketones in your liver. Saturated fats are harder to burn, and do not send your body into ketosis.

You want to also make sure you are eating protein as well, as this helps your body stay strong throughout the day as it is filling as well. Without carbs, you may find that your body tries to go on a hunger strike, so make sure that you are eating plenty of protein as well. Protein also has a good fat content as well.

Keep your carbs under a hundred grams a day. A few carbs are okay, just try to eat twice as much protein and fat.

The keto diet is literally a diet in which you switch one type of calorie with another. In this case, you are switching carbs with fats, and even though it seems counter-intuitive, it is actually quite genius. You figure out how much you are consuming by counting your calories via macronutrients, which are the sections of calories that you need to have a balanced diet.

Exercise

Exercise actually helps keep your mind sharp, because it also helps you burn fat and keep your body in ketosis. You do not have to get an expensive gym membership; thirty minutes a day of light cardio should do the trick as well.

The more you exercise, however, the more fat you burn. The more fat you burn, the stronger your memory will get. The ketones you will be burning in your liver will help your brain function and keep your mind sharp.

Plus, exercise is a great time to think about things through the day. You can try to recall a memory from that day, and see how much you remember. This game is great for those who want to be able to remember their day with ease.

Reduce Stress

Have you ever been so stressed that you felt like you could not remember anything? Stress is known to affect your memory by causing you to focus only on what you are stressed about. This leads to you forgetting important things because your brain is not able to pay attention.

Play Memory Games

It may seem silly, but those matching memory games are really good for your visual memory. You know, the ones that you played as a little kid where you flipped a card over and tried to match it with another card by remembering the placement of that card? This game is good for you well into adulthood as it helps keep your memory sharp.

You can also play auditory memory games. There are several that have you listen to a sound, and then they show you something, and you have to remember the sound after seeing a picture that is unrelated to the sound. This is great for your auditory memory.

There are not many haptic memory games, however, because haptic senses are harder to create a game. Especially if the game is on a computer.

You can find a lot of these games online for free, so don't hesitate to check them out!

Chapter 2: Thinking and Problem Solving

Thought is viewed to be abstract. There is no real way to track how it works, as not everyone thinks in the same fashion. Even scans show the differences in parts of the brain that are used when thinking.

However, it is important to know how to keep your train of thought and strengthen your mind to focus better. This will be touched upon in the next chapter.

When you are thinking, it allows you to process the information you are taking in. If you were not to think, you would only act, and that could cause a lot of issues.

Psychology

Thought is designed to help people figure out what they are going to do before they try to do it. It is seen as an evolutionary aspect, as humans are the only ones to think before doing anything. Perhaps it was for species preservation, but no one truly knows. It is all theories at this point.

However, there are ways you can improve your ability to think things through if that is what you are looking to do. This is the only way that has been proven to improve your thought, and it is something that a lot of people groan about when they come across it. Problem-solving.

Use Problem Solving.

Have you ever found yourself in a difficult situation, and you are not sure where to turn? Have you found yourself wondering how to solve a certain problem? Do you often question your ability to think things through clearly? Don't fret, because you are not alone. Millions of people struggle with the ability to problem solve. However, there are ways to improve your skills.

You may be wondering what problem-solving has to do with thinking, and the answer is simple: Problem-solving forces you to use the power of thought to open your mind to the answer that may not be out in the open. By working on your problem-solving skills, you exercise your brain, which has been proven to help people think more clearly and helps them organize the thoughts that run through their mind.

Definition

Problem-solving comes with different definitions. However, at this moment, the one we will be using here is the one that is referring to common human problem-solving, not the computerized and digital problem-solving. We will define problem-solving as an act of finding out a solution to difficult, usually confusing, situations by analyzing multiple steps and by going through a process to defeat or overcome an obstacle.

Problem-solving strategies

Problem-solving, in the simplest form, is viewed as a cycle. The process goes like this: you analyze the problem, think deeply for a solution, try the solution, modify the errors, and then get the solution for the problem. And then, you have to start all over again when there is a new problem that will arise. We may not notice it, but we're doing this every day such as when deciding what to wear, searching a detour around a construction area on our way to office or work, and thinking about what we will have for lunch or dinner.

There are many different ways to look at problem-solving. If you are a math person, problem-solving probably comes to you best in mathematical form. If you are a science person, you probably approach it like the scientific method.

There is no tried and true method of improving your skills. However, there are several that are known to help, and trying them can't hurt. You are bound to find something that works for you. If you don't, that alone could be a test of your problem-solving skills, and you could try to find what works for you!

Tips for Improving Your Problem Solving Skills.

1. **Dance**

"There is no way dancing could in any way affect your brain." If you think this statement is true, you would be absolutely incorrect. Dancing is a great way to work on your problem-solving skills. Have you ever tried to dance? You have to coordinate each step to the beat of the music, and if you have a particularly difficult transition, then you have to figure out the best way to move through it without tripping yourself up. It is also great exercise, which is good for the brain.

Dancing burns ketones in your liver, which functions as food for your brain. This will help you brainstorm like a pro, and really get to show off what that brain of yours can do.

2. Work out Your Brain

"Logic games are for children. Adults are too old to play silly games." Another incorrect statement. Logic games stimulate your brain and help exercise it. You see, your brain is a muscle as well as an organ, and if you do not exercise it, it begins to get weak. Logic games help keep your mind sharp, and they can be fun as well. There is nothing childish about being on top of your mental strength.

It is important to exercise your brain, along with your body to really give yourself the best chance at having a strong mind to amp up your thought processes.

3. Put on the Tunes and Move

"Music is a distraction, and will get in the way." Look at us, clearing up misconceptions one myth at a time. It is actually scientifically proven that music helps stimulate brain function. That coupled with exercise is a double threat and thinking about a difficult problem to make it a triple threat. Although physical workouts can help you think more focused and get your blood flowing to your brain, it still does not necessarily help you solve a problem, nor it improves your skills in problem-solving. However, when you add music to your exercise, you add another thing in the background which forces your mind to focus more. Thus, music can help you increase and improve your problem-solving skills significantly.

Even if you are not working out, put on some music and try to do some logic puzzles. The music will pull your mind in a different direction, making it harder for you to concentrate, thus strengthening your problem-solving skills that much more efficiently.

4. Keeping a journal

"Only teenage girls keep journals." Misconceptions everywhere. The truth is, some of the most renowned scientists and intellectuals keep journals in order to organize their often eccentric thoughts. It is impossible to remember every fleeting thought that passes through your mind, but if you write them down, you don't have to.

Journals are great for brainstorming as well. You can jot down all of your ideas that you are having and be able to pick the best one by comparing them. This is a great problem-solving tool.

6. Distance yourself from the problem

"If I am distant from a problem, it will be harder to solve." This is the opposite of correct. When you are too close to a problem, you create a barrier between the solution and your own mind. You have to take a step back so you can look at it from all angles.

It can be hard to look at a personal problem objectively. However, if you get too caught up in the problem, it can make it harder to find the best solution, because you will be biased about what to do or say to get the problem fixed. While in the long run, you may fix the problem, you can overlook a smarter and more efficient way to finish it up.

Chapter 3: Learning and Attention Performance

You know the phrase "you learn something new every day"? It is honestly true. Every day you take in new information, and that is exactly what learning is. Learning is the act of taking in information that has already been processed. You can learn through play, teaching or rote. However, teaching is actually the least effective way to learn. Many people have to experience the information first hand.

People learn in a way that is far different than animals do. While animals learn from extensive training, human learn mostly through education. Someone would teach them what he or she needs to know. Commonly, learning occurs outside the comfort of the home.

Rote learning

One of the most common ways that humans learn is through rote learning. This is the act of memorizing something. There is a special way you go about memorizing the information though. You have to write it down, say it, and see the information. The idea is that the more you handle the information, the more you will remember.

Not everyone learns the same way, which makes it difficult to pinpoint a specific way to help you learn with ease. However, improving your attention span will help increase your learning abilities a bit, as you will be able to focus more on the information you are learning.

A lot of people have a hard time focusing, so they find that they have to work harder to get their work done. However, there are ways to improve your attention span and focus, and here are some tips.

How to Improve Your Attention Span and Focus

Many people struggle day in and day out with being able to focus on their daily tasks properly. If you are one of these people, you are not alone, and there are other people in the world who are going through the same problem. In fact, over eighty percent of the world's population has trouble concentrating from time to time in varying degrees.

Some people have problems focusing daily, while others tend only to have problems if they have a lot on their plates. No matter the reason, you can beat the distractions and regain laser-like focus just by knowing how it works, and have some tips on how to keep yourself on track.

Environment

If you are in an office space. Chances are your surroundings are very boring. Some people can work well in boring scenery, and others need something to break the monotony to keep their mind from wandering. Even if you can work in a boring workstation, personalizing your space a bit may boost your morale on days where you are a little stressed, thus allowing you to leave your stress behind and work harder and focus better.

5. Be comfortable: If you need to bring in your own office chair, do so. Comfort is the number one contributor and detractor for focus. You have to be comfortable so that you do not constantly have to break concentration to move around. If you are comfortable, you will be able to focus well, as you do not have to move at all.

6. Add pictures: Pictures can break up the monotony of your boring space. If you are a college student,

your desk is probably where you spend your life learning, so why not adorn the walls around it with some motivational landscapes or some pictures of things you enjoy. This will break the monotony and give you something to look at to keep your mind from wandering. Just stay away from pictures that have words as those can be distracting.

7. Detour the noise: earplugs, earphones, and other sound canceling objects are a gift from heaven. These things keep you concentrating on your work, rather than the world around you. If you are in a noisy environment, try putting on some headphones and playing some classical music to drown out the world around you. Classical music is great to help you learn because it opens your mind. Try it out sometime.

Nutrition

The famous mantra says you are what you eat. What you put into your digestive system will affect your ability to focus. Your diet plays a huge role in your brain's functionality. If your brain does not receive the proper nutrition it needs, then it will not function properly as it should.

3. Drink water: Your brain needs you to stay hydrated in order for it to properly function. If you are dehydrated, it makes it harder for you to focus, because your brain is starting to shut down to preserve itself. If you don't drink enough water, it is equivalent to literally drying out your brain. If you don't think that sounds scary, I am not sure what would scare you.

4. Eat breakfast: Have you ever been really hungry? Did it make you have a hard time focusing? Hunger is one of the largest focus detractors there are. Your body needs food to function, and as a defense, when you get to a certain point food becomes all you can think about. It is best to start your day off right with a balanced breakfast so your body can make it to lunch and your mind can stay on track.

5. Get up and move around: Digestion of food can be an uncomfortable process, so don't be afraid to aid it

by moving. This will also help get more blood flowing to your brain. While moving around too much can distract you, taking a quick walk will help you get your mind clear and ready to learn.

Mindset

Mind over matter is another way to handle focus difficulties. Even if you have a problem with concentrating due to a disorder, you can still improve your focus by taking control of your mind. This will allow you to focus more than you ever thought was possible.

9. *Set aside time to deal with worries*: Worrying and anxiety is the number one killer of productivity. Worrying too much can kill your thoughts throughout the day, making focusing tedious and wearisome. Later in this book, we will learn how to balance work and homelife that will help you focus better.

10. *Focus on one task at a time*: This may seem to go against everything that you know. However, the truth is, it is harder to learn when you are multitasking. This is because your focus is divided

amongst different things, and you cannot truly give your undivided attention to what you need to be focusing on primarily. Focusing on one task at a time will help you absorb more information from the subjects you are trying to learn.

11. *Close your email box and chat program*: When you are trying to learn new material, it can be tempting to take that time to also answer messages from people you know. However, that detracts from the time you have to learn what you are trying to learn. Shut down the phone, and turn off your notifications on your laptop. Just focus on the task at hand. If you take the time to really focus on what you are learning, you will find you absorb so much more information.

12. *Prioritize*: Not know what to do next can kill your focus because it will eat your time figuring out what task to do next. It will stress your brain to remember things that you should not miss or forget. To avoid this, spend a little time in the morning to plan ahead your day. Make a list of what needs to prioritize and how to finish each task.

13. *Switch between high- and low-priority tasks*: Many people prioritize their tasks at work from high to low. They work on the more important projects and leave the low-priority projects for last. This might seem effective for some people, but it can actually bog you down causing your brain to lose focus when starting to work on the projects that have low importance. By alternating high and low tasks, you give your brain a break making you focus longer. Thus, it will allow you to finish tasks in less time.

More Tips for Improving Your Concentration

- *Take short breaks*: Have you ever had cram session, and then found that you couldn't remember a thing you read. This is actually a pretty common occurrence. Your brain needs time to rest. Just like with a machine, sometimes you have to give it time to cool down. They can't run 24/7. You are only human. Give yourself a schedule where you study for an hour and take a five to ten-minute break. This will allow your brain to rest and reset so you can retain more information.

- *Do your hardest tasks when you're most alert*: Don't save that cram session for last minute before the big test. Do your bulk studying after breakfast. This is when your brain is typically the most alert, and you have the best chance to remember everything you studied. Saving these study sessions for when you are so tired all you can think about is sleep will kill your memory and make it harder to learn.

- Look busy: Find something that will make you look busy. Perhaps put a do not disturb sign up or wear a phone headset. This way people will know not to disturb you. If you look like you are busy, many people will wait until you are not busy to ask you a question, which allows you to learn in peace.

- Promise yourself a reward: Self-rewards is a great way to stay motivated to focus. It can be simple such as work for an hour and get a snack from the vending machine if you are successful. The trick is to hold yourself accountable if you do not meet your goal. No goal, no reward.

- Schedule email downloads: The reality is, emails do come in, for unknown reasons, at the most inconvenient times. This may be common, but it can actually distract your focus especially when you get tempted to check the emails constantly. If so, you should set a time within your day to answer emails. Once you set on a specific schedule, train yourself to download emails only at that specific period of time.

Think of Your Mind as a Muscle

Your mind is not just a typical body organ. It is also a working muscle, an essential one. It can work with heavy workloads just as how your arms and back can, except your mind works mentally rather than physically.

What do you think would happen if you did not exercise your brain? If you think nothing would change, that is where you are wrong. Many people have the misconception that their brain will function the same forever, and that is why dementia and Alzheimer's are so devastating and tragic in our eyes. You see it as an unavoidable tragedy, but the truth is, they can be avoided if you treat your mind like a muscle. Work it out, and feed it the right nutrition.

Think of your day as a workout for your brain. Do you go to the gym every day and just focus on your chest? No. You most likely rotate your exercises in a pattern so that every part of your body gets a workout. You should do the same with your mind. Find different exercises for your brain and cycle through them.

Just as how you can hit a wall with a workout, so you can with your concentration. When hitting this wall, you simply have to dig a deeper to sought the motivation that will push through. A promise of reward can help. Nevertheless, working hard will strengthen your brain – your memory. Here are some useful tips that will definitely help you do just that:

Fighting for Attention

Technology can both save and destroy our attention spans. While there are apps you can use that silence your phone during times where you need to focus, a lot of people do not have the will power to do so with vigor. Many people will find themselves turning off this app and going back to using their phones and being distracted.

Humans are easily distracted creatures. That is why robots are so popular. They can do twice the work most humans can because they do not get distracted. As a whole, the human race could seriously use some work on their attention skills.

Of course, if you are reading this, you probably want to improve all of your cognitive skills. Whether it may be to combat the robots, or just to get through the work day, it is good that you want to fight the technology blues and get back to a strong mind.

One of the easiest ways to get a strong attention span is to go zen. Zen is where you get so lost in your work that you forget the world around you even exists. This is a wonderful thing because when you are in that state, you forget your troubles and your worries. It may seem a little strange that you want to get lost in your work that much, but it can make the time go faster, and you can learn so much more because at that moment it is just you and your information.

Meditation is a great way to help yourself achieve a zen state of mind. Meditation involves getting out of your body and into your mind. You do not have to sit cross legged and mutter "hmmm, " but you do have to be comfortable enough to let your body move over so you can enter your own brain.

When you meditate, you will have a moment where it seems like everything on your body itches. You will have the urge to scratch everywhere. Your body likes to be the center of attention. Ignore it, and it will grudgingly allow your mind to take over. Once you are in this state, you can focus more clearly on your work. From there you will find the clarity of mind that you have is out of this world, and you will learn so much more.

Everyone faces the struggle of maintaining focus. That is normal and is something that you should not be ashamed of. However, if it regularly causes you delay with your work, then you should probably strive to become better at focusing. This chapter contains a bunch of tips that will help you do so. These tips are even more perfect for people who struggle with attention deficiency.

Everyone struggles from time to time when it comes to maintaining focus. That is nothing to be ashamed of. However, if it regularly impedes with your work, then you should strive to become better at focusing. This entire chapter is filled with tips on how to do so, and here are even more. These tips are for people who struggle with attention deficiency.

PART IV

CHAPTER ONE

A WARNING

Everybody is different, making every habit different. That means that all these tips coming up are subjective. It's not something that will work for everybody. Another thing you need to be aware of is that your habit could be something more. I'm going to go over this possible problem quickly. Keep in mind this is not to cure or diagnose you with anything. If you think you may have a psychological disorder, as opposed to a bad habit, please seek medical attention.

For your information, a habit is defined as a settled or regular tendency or practice; especially one that is hard to give up.

OCD, obsessive compulsive disorder, can be confused as a habit. OCD can fall into four main categories;

- checking

- contamination/mental contamination

- hoarding

- ruminations/intrusive thoughts

OCD is diagnosed by when obsessions and compulsions:

- Consume excessive amounts of time

- Causes significant distress

- Interferes with daily functions

Your habit, itself, could be OCD, or your inability to break the habit, could be caused by OCD. An example of OCD being the habit would be hoarding. An example of OCD interfering your ability to break a habit would be intrusive thoughts. Now, when breaking a habit you will have intrusive thoughts, but they should just come and go. If your intrusive thoughts are constant and interfere with your life, then OCD could be a factor.

Other psychological disorders that could be confused with a habit are, eating disorders. Anorexia nervosa and bulimia nervosa are common eating disorders where people end up starving themselves or binging and purging. A lesser known eating disorder, which is the one most likely to be confused as a habit, is a binge-eating disorder.

With binge-eating disorder, people lose control of their eating habits. Unlike with bulimia nervosa, periods of binges are not followed by purging, which is why most people with binge-eating disorder are overweight. It is the top eating disorder in the US. Symptoms of binge-eating disorder are:

- Eating an unusually large amount of food in a specific amount of time

- Eating even when you're full or not hungry

- Eating fast during binge episodes

- Eating until you are uncomfortably full

- Eating alone or in secret to avoid embarrassment

- Feeling distressed, ashamed, or guilty when not eating

- Frequent dieting, possibly without weight loss

Chances are everybody can say that they have experienced one or more of these symptoms. For example, most holidays' people will over eat. That does not mean you have binge-eating disorder. Keep in mind disorders interrupt your everyday life, and happen constantly.

If you just overeat when watching TV, or when you're bored, then you probably don't have a disorder. If you are concerned that you might, then please seek medical advice.

Make sure that if you think you have a disorder to see your doctor make sure. It's better to believe you have a disease than go around with an undiagnosed disorder. I want to make sure that you can live the life you deserve and making sure that your habit isn't something more serious is important.

CHAPTER TWO

A HISTORY OF HABITS

Imagine this; your alarm goes off. You slide out of bed and slump your way to the bathroom. You do your business and then hop in the shower. Once finished you brush your teeth before you get dressed. Once dressed you head to the kitchen to have your coffee and breakfast. Now, what just happened? You were on complete autopilot. You are so used to doing the same thing every morning you don't have to think about it. That is what a habit is.

Human beings are creatures of habit. We get into a routine, and we stick to it. Then it becomes a struggle to change.

Chances are your habits are caused by stress or boredom. You start doing things to distract your brain from the stress or boredom, giving you brain a brief moment of utopia.

Stress and boredom aren't just triggers for certain habits. They're triggers for most habits. Whether you have a problem with eating, smoking, biting your nails, or spending mindless hours on the computer, whatever it may be you're using the habit to suppress those emotions. There is a chance that a deeper issue causes the stress or boredom that is being felt.

Ask yourself, is there a belief or a reason you're holding onto this habit?

The key to overcoming a habit is to figure out what is causing it. Did something happen when you were younger? Do you believe something bad is going to happen if you stop?

That's why there is no one solution. Take the habit of smoking. According to the World Health Organization, more than one billion people smoke. Most of those people are smoking for different reasons. Some may smoke because they saw their parents smoke, or their friends. They may have started smoking as a way to cope with stress.

A Loop

Every habit begins with a psychological pattern. The habit loop is a three-part process. It begins with a trigger. The trigger tells you brain to go into automatic mode and let a behavior happen. The second part is the routine which is the actual habit itself. The last part is the reward. The reward is something your brain likes and helps it remember the loop in the future.

According to neuroscientists, habit-making behaviors are controlled in the basal ganglia. The basal ganglia are also the area of the brain that controls emotions, memories, and patterns. As stated above, a habit is a pattern.

Decisions are controlled in the prefrontal cortex. A habit starts as a behavior or decision, but the more you do it, the less the brain works. The decision-making part of your brain goes to sleep. That's what makes multitasking possible.

Good habits are programmed the same as bad habits are. A good habit, such as brushing your teeth, gets programmed by repetition just like smoking. Or learning to parallel park works the same as overeating.

The fact that they work the same is a good thing. That makes it easier for you to retrain your brain.

Problems

There are going to be problems when trying to break a habit, especially if your habit involves any stimulant. At that point, you're not just trying to stop the habit, but also working through the detox symptoms. For example, nicotine, via tobacco, is one of the most heavily consumed drugs in the world. In Australia, smoking is one of the biggest causes of, preventable, death, killing about 15,000 people per year. It's also one of the hardest to quit. Withdrawal from nicotine can cause insomnia, irritability, anxiety, and difficulty concentrating.

Slip-ups are inevitable, but if you're working to break a habit that involves any stimulating drug, it's going to be a lot harder. This could include smoking, drinking, even coffee. Keep this in the back of your mind so that you are prepared.

CHAPTER THREE

A HABITS HABITAT

Necessarily true. You can control your habits, but your environment plays a huge part of what you do on a daily basis. One of your brain's primary functions is to find and use patterns as shortcuts to process the information we're presented with on a daily basis.

In a study conducted on habits vs. intentions, researchers found that students that switched Universities were more likely to change their daily habits. Those habits were easier to change than they were for the control group because they weren't exposed to familiar daily cues. This can be seen in every bad habit that somebody has.

Eating Habits

Have you ever been driving home from work, not thinking about food, when you see your favorite fast food joint, and suddenly your start craving a cheeseburger? It's not your fault. Everybody experiences moments like that.

Our food environment is broken down into two categories; the atmosphere we encounter when eating, and how food is portioned. The cues vary from what's being eaten, its packaging or utensil size, and the amount of food. Think about when you eat out. You will undoubtedly receive a huge plate of food. You don't think you can eat it all, but then you end up cleaning your plate. Seeing an empty plate signals satiety in our brains.

Maybe eating at home will help you avoid these triggers. Not so fast. Home plate sizes have increased 22% over the last century. Where you store your food also plays a large part in your eating habits, bringing new meaning to "Out of sight, out of mind."

Don't worry though. There are ways to overcome these triggers.

- First, choose smaller plates to use at home. It takes less food to fill up a small plate. You're eating less, but you're still cleaning your plate and making your brain happy.

- Another way is to pre-portion your food. Have everything portioned out into single servings.

- It also helps to focus on one thing at a time. When you're eating, only concentrate on eating. Try not to watch TV or the computer while you're eating.

- Most importantly learn the true signs of hunger and avoid mindless eating. This comes in handy when you're not in control of the food.

Smoking Habits

Environmental triggers for smokers can be harder to break than triggers for overeaters. According to the American Psychological Association is in an area associated with smoking can cause a smoker to have a craving. That means they could walk into a bar where there are no cigarettes, ashtrays, or other smokers, yet still, have a craving because they associate the setting with smoking.

Your regular daily routine could also cause triggers. Some people associate their morning cup of coffee with smoking. An easy fix for that is to keep yourself busy in the morning. Try to distract yourself from the craving. You can also trade your coffee out for tea or juice.

Most smokers smoke while driving making the car another common trigger. If you have cravings whenever you drive try singing along to the radio or a CD. You could also substitute smoking with chewing gum while driving.

Stress is another major trigger for smokers. Cigarettes have thousands of chemicals in them that trick your brain into thinking that they are helping relieve your stress. The key to overcoming the stress trigger is to find new ways to relieve your stress. Meditation and yoga are both good stress management techniques.

Drinking Habits

Stress and anxiety are big triggers for drinking. As I mentioned earlier, they are also the cause for most habits.

There are two main types of triggers; external and internal. External are people, places, or things that trigger you desire to drink. They are easier to avoid than internal triggers. Internal triggers are, as the name states, inner emotions that trigger your desire to drink.

A good way to figure out exactly what causes your triggers is to track them for a week. Keep a journal with you and every time you have the urge to drink, write down what happened or where you were that caused the urge.

Some simple ways to avoid external triggers are to keep little, to no alcohol, at home. Socially, try avoiding situations that involve drinking. You may feel guilty turning down invitations to go out with your friends, but just remember it's not forever. You only have to turn them down until your urges become more manageable.

It won't be possible to stay away from all triggers. Always remind yourself why you are making this change. Keep a list somewhere on your person that you can read when you have the urge to drink. Talk to an accountability partner. That's what they're there for. Distract yourself. Find something to do to keep your mind off your urge.

Lastly, you could also ride it out. Problem the hardest, but tell yourself that it's only temporary. That the feeling will pass.

Using your Triggers

You can also use your triggers for good. Task association is a good way to control your triggers. For instance, doctors have helped insomniacs by telling them to only go to bed when they are sleepy. If they can't sleep, they are told to go to a different room that way their bed is only associated with sleep. This could work to cut back on environmental triggers.

Instead of keeping snacks close to your work area, keep them in the kitchen or break room. That way you associate your desk with working and not with eating. Train yourself to associate your car with singing along with the radio instead of smoking. Only eat at the kitchen table and not on the couch. That way the couch is only for watching TV and the kitchen table is for eating.

CHAPTER FOUR

A SIMPLE BREAk

I'm going to start with the most basic three steps of breaking a bad habit. I don't want to overload you with a bunch of information. These first three basic steps will give you the building blocks to move onto more in-depth information.

The first step you have to take in breaking a habit is the decision to break the habit. You're probably thinking, "Duh," but you have to make sure you have a reason. If you don't have a reason to quit, you will not quit. You won't get anywhere if you go at this thinking you "might" have something you need to change. You have to know and want to change. Make a list of the reasons why you want to stop. If you can't think of anything, make a list of the bad things that will happen if you don't stop. For example, if you don't stop binge eating you could become overweight and develop serious health problems.

The next step is to be ready to face your boredom or emotions. As mentioned before habits are formed out of boredom or stress. You have to be willing to take a look at your life and figure out how to change what is causing your dissatisfaction. You must be ready to face the discomfort. We as humans don't like discomfort, but if you can overcome that, then you have surpassed one of the biggest hurdles. Make your life the way you want it to be.

The last step is to find a new way to relieve stress. You could have the life of your dreams, but you still suffer from stress. You feel stressed, so you turn to alcohol. You drink, and then you don't feel stressed. That makes you think you have everything together. Instead, you need to replace you drinking with something new, something healthy. You could use meditation or exercise as a healthy alternative. The first three steps are:

1. Make sure you have a good reason to break your habit

2. Be ready to face the emotions and boredom that is causing your habit

3. Find a new way to handle your stress

Starting with these three steps will put you well on your way to breaking your bad habit. In the coming chapters, I will go into more detail on how to switch out your bad habits for new healthy habits.

A Big Break

As learned in the last chapter, there are three necessary steps to breaking habits. While those three steps are paramount there are other tips and tricks to take your habit breaking to the next level. We'll discuss several of them in this chapter, and flesh out even more throughout the rest of the book. A big part of break a bad habit is replacing it with a new one; I'll wait until later to explain how to start said new habit. Now, let's look at some tips to kick those habits to the curb.

1. Set a Start Date

Mark it on your calendar when you want to start changing your habit. You have to be serious about this, so having a countdown will help you to stay on track. The countdown will help to create excitement. Just like a child counting down the 25 to Christmas, or the days before their birthday. You want to drastically change your life for the better, so there should be an element of excitement.

2. Bait and Switch

Once you know what habit you want to change then, you can sub a new habit, temporary or permanent, in its place. If you're a nail-biter, try subbing in gum. Gum can also be used to help with smoking urges.

3. Discover your triggers

Knowing why we make certain decisions is the key to conquering your habits. Often we perform the habit without even realizing we're doing it. That's why it's called a habit. For a long time after my Dad quit smoking, every time he got in the car he would roll down the window and fiddle with his pocket because that's what he would do when he smoked. He never even realized he was doing that until we told him. But you can fix that by being consciously aware of when you perform your habit. There are five main triggers for habits; location, time, emotional state, other people, and an immediately preceding action. Start to take notes whenever you perform the bad habit. Soon you will be able to figure out what is triggering your problem.

4. Don't go cold turkey

Everybody has probably tried to give up something cold turkey. Cold turkey is a favorite of smokers, but it rarely ever works. It's similar to telling a child to not do something, and that will be exactly what they go and do. Cold turkey is centered on perfection. People think that they if they slip up then they have failed. Nobody is perfect. Cold Turkey leaves no wiggle room, and with something like this, you need a little wiggle room.

5. Switch up your environment

You don't have to move or do anything drastic. The smallest change can switch your brain's thinking. You always smoke in the parking lot at work; the parking lot becomes a trigger. If you change your routine just slightly you will trick your brain into not craving a cigarette. You can also use the 20-second rule. Make it so that it takes 20 more seconds for you to make your habit. If you smoke, keep your cigarettes in a draw where you have to walk to get them. If you have a problem with snacking, put your snacks in the back of the pantry.

6. Make it incremental

The best way to make a change is to set daily incremental changes. You need to wean yourself off of you habit. The first step is to establish a baseline. This is going to differ according to what you want to change. Such as; how much time you watch TV, how many cigarettes you smoke each day, how many drinks you consume when out with friends. Then choose how much you're going to give up each week. If you're a smoker and you typically smoke a whole pack a day; then the first week or two you go to 15. Then the next two weeks you go down to 10, and so on until you stop smoking.

7. Don't focus on what you don't want

Most everybody that makes a goal will make this mistake. They will say, I'm not going to do this, or I'm not going to that. Setting a goal like that is setting you up for failure. Instead, decide what you are going to do. It's similar to the bait and switch. If you know you like to snack when working; instead of saying you're not going to snack, say you are going to snack on vegetables. Then all you have to do is switch your chips out for carrots.

8.   Do it in honor of yourself

Research shows that people that try to break habits out of frustration or guilt will ultimately fail. People that respect themselves and are happy with who they are will be more successful. Work to change your bad habit from a position of personal strength and confidence.

9.   Make a declaration

Social media has become a big part of most everybody's day. Use this to your advantage. Announce on social media the change you are going to make if you feel comfortable doing so. Then keep them updated as you progress. Chances are you will have friends that will congratulate you, and that will make you feel good about what you are doing. This one, of course, isn't for everybody. Some habits that you are trying to break may not be something you want to share with the whole world. Some habits are very personal, so if you don't feel comfortable sharing it with a large group of people, then you don't have to. Keep in mind though having somebody to talk to can help you along the way.

10. Be prepared to forgive yourself

There will be slip-ups. We are only human beings, and we learn from out slip ups. When you slip up, forgive yourself. Wake up the next day ready to beat your habit. Don't go at it with an all or nothing attitude. There are no scorecards in life. The slip up happened, learn from it, and move on. If you are serious about beating this habit, you won't throw your hands up in defeat after a few lapses.

Classical Conditioning

Classical conditioning is a psychological learning process that occurs when two stimuli are repeatedly paired; a response that is at first elicited by the second stimulus is eventually elicited by the first stimulus alone. An example of this is Pavlov's dog.

Pavlov trained his dog to associate the thrill of being fed with the sound of a bell. He would ring a bell every time he gave the dogs their food. After several repeats of this the dog associated the sound of the bell with receiving food. The dogs would then begin to salivate every time they heard the bell.

This theory doesn't just apply to salivating dogs. Over the years it has formed an important rationale for the development, maintenance, and a relapse of bad habits.

Habits work much in the same way as Pavlov's dogs did. For a smoker, just the site of a pack of cigarettes will elicit a dopamine response causing them to have the urge to smoke. This isn't restricted to smokers either. The same dopamine response happens in alcoholics, overeaters, and so on.

This can be used in reverse, to break a habit. The bell was the trigger for the dogs to start salivating because they knew the food was coming. Just like if a smoker always lights up when they get in the car. The car is the trigger for the smoker to want to smoke. If you start ringing the bell for the dog but don't give them food they will eventually learn that the bell no longer means food. If you stop lighting up every time you get in the car eventually you won't have that trigger anymore.

This is definitely one of the more complicated and harder ways of breaking a habit, but it will work. All the rest have ways of distracting your brain, making it easier to change.

Procrastination

Everybody has been faced with procrastination at some point. It can also be detrimental in your ability to break a habit. But just like breaking a habit, you can overcome procrastination.

In a nutshell, procrastination is when you continually put off doing something. The first step, like with most things, is **realizing you are procrastinating**. If you're honest with yourself, then you know when you are procrastinating, but if you're not sure here are some ways to know;

- Waiting for the right mood, or day to start something

- Doing unimportant tasks to avoid what you need to be doing

- Sitting down to start working, then immediately going to do something else

Once you've realized you are procrastinating, then you can move onto the next step.

Figure out why you are procrastinating. It could be either you or the task. You might find the task unpleasant. Which, since you're changing a habit, you probably will find the task unpleasant. You could also be disorganized or overwhelmed. An important part of the habit breaking process is being organized and knowing what you are doing. Another reason could be that your heart is not into it. You don't have a good enough reason to change this habit.

Lastly, **adopt anti-procrastination strategies**. Procrastination itself is a habit. As you've learned, the only way of getting rid of a habit is persistently not doing the habit. The same tricks you have or will learn about breaking a habit will work to keep you from procrastination. Set up a reward system. Have somebody check in with you. Anything that will keep you accountable in some way, shape, or form.

Be Prepared

Unfortunately, a fact of the world is there will be people that want to sabotage you and your goals. It's not bad enough that you will have self-Sabotaging moments, but you will have to handle other people trying to do the same thing. You have to be prepared to ignore them. They may or may not know what they're doing. Their words can be poison to your success. The moment you start taking their words of "advice" will be your first steps towards failure. Having a plan to handle naysayers is just as important to know what you'll do when you have urges. Make sure you know what to say or do when negative   comments   arise.

CHAPTER FIVE

A NEW YEAR'S PROBLEM

What's something you get asked every New Year? What's your New Year's resolution? For the first few weeks of the year, every person you see will ask you the same thing. It's expected of everybody to make a New Year's resolution, yet they don't work for people. At least not the way people use them. There's a saying that the definition of insanity is doing the same over and over and again expecting a different result. Then why do people continue to try to make and keep a resolution? People think that resolutions will help them to break some of their bad habits. First, let's look at why a resolution does not work.

1. You're setting the wrong goals.

The most common resolution is to lose weight or get in shape. You wake up the first of January, hop out of bed and say, "I'm going lose 50 pounds this year." By the 15th of January, when you're supposed to be at the gym, you're watching reruns of "The Big Bang Theory" while eating a pint of rocky road. You did nothing wrong. Keeping goals takes more thought than just stating them. These types of goals have little to no leeway. When something happens, and you fail, you will be less likely to make more in the future.

2. Your resolution rarely has to do with the real problem.

You decide to run out and get that gym membership on January first. Good luck fighting the crowd. The gym is going to be packed with everybody else just like you. Once you're in there, you start comparing yourself to everybody. It will definitely help you work through deep-seated psychological issues with inadequacy, rejection, competitiveness and insecurity, but it won't help you solve the real problem. If your goal is to be healthier, then the gym might help, but if you have a problem overeating then it's not going to help. More than likely you're still coming home and eating all the calories you burned off earlier.

3. You set too many.

When making a New Year's resolution a lot of people will think, "While I'm changing this I'll go ahead a change this." Their list of resolutions ends up looking like this;

- Be a better person

- Lose weight

- Sleep more

- Learn a new language

- Drink less

And so on. I get stressed just looking at the list. Our body, as it is, is in homeostasis. It's happy and doesn't want to be changed. The brain has only a finite amount of willpower, and if you start trying to change too many things at once, the brain becomes overwhelmed. The first two weeks of keeping your 10 resolutions may go well, but then your brain starts to smoke and eventually just stops. Then you fall back into old habits.

4. They're too vague.

Let's look at the list above again.

- Be a better person

- Lose weight

- Sleep more

- Learn a new language

- Drink less

They all have something in common. They're about as clear as muddy water. There is no definite way to know if you passed or failed. It's like you teacher gave you an okay on your report card instead of an A or B.

- I want to learn a new language- Great, but what language? Are you trying to learn all languages or a specific one? How are you going to learn your new language? You have no definite plan on how to learn that mysterious new language.

- I want to lose weight- Alright, but how much? Are you overweight and you want to get to a healthier BMI? Do you just want to lose an extra five pounds to fit back into that old dress? You approach those options in very different ways. You have to know how much and why you want to lose weight.

- I want to be a better person- That's admirable, but how? How do you want to be a better person? Do you have a bad temper? Do you use your phone too much? In what way to you want to change? It's great you want to be a better person, but you have to know what aspect of you that you need to change to achieve that goal.

With this new information as to why New Year's resolutions have a tendency to fail, we can now discover how to make them work. No need to swear them off, instead learn how to make them so that you will actually keep them.

1. Be the person you want to be.

The key to keeping any goal is to imagine that you have already achieved your goal. Don't just say, "I'm going to lose weight," or, "I'm going to stop smoking." Be that person. Visualize you eating healthier and working out regularly. Everybody knows the saying "fake it till you make it," this is the same concept. The more you believe on the inside you are already there, the more it will show on the outside.

2. Make them simple.

In fact make them so stupid simple that completing one seems too easy. Remember the acronym KISS, keep it simple stupid. The simpler the goal is, the easier it is to tell that you have accomplished something.

- If you want to drink less hold yourself to drinking one less drink each day, or each week. Then the next week cut out another drink. Continue doing just that, each week, until you reach your overall goal. You'll know you're achieving your goal when you drink less this week than you did the last.

- If you want to sleep more, start setting the alarm to go to bed. If you typically go to bed at midnight, set the alarm on your phone to go off at 10:30 telling you to get ready for bed. That way you will be in bed by eleven. You'll start waking up more refreshed, and you will quickly see that you're achieving your goals.

- If you want to lose weight set your goal to eat more fruits and vegetables each week. Instead of have French fries with your burger have carrot sticks. Start switching out the high-fat sides with whole veggies. You will start seeing a significant change, and you will know you're achieving your goals.

3. Make yourself more accountable.

When people set a resolution, there's nothing that happens to them if they fail, besides the fact that they don't achieve their goal. Instead of having an easy way out, make it painful to not succeed. Dietbet.com is a website that will help you do just that. They have helped over 150,000 people achieve their weight loss goals. The way it works is you choose one of their plans, which you have to pay for. If you achieve your goal, you will win a part of the pot, the money you put in plus some. If you don't achieve your goal, you get nothing. Of course, you don't need their website to do the same thing. If your goal is to quit smoking tell everybody that if you smoke a cigarette, you will pay x amount of dollars to an acquaintance/co-worker/charity that you don't like. Not only are you giving to something or someone you don't like, but you are also spending money that you could use for something you want or need.

4. Keep the number down.

You probably have a million things you want to change, but you have to narrow down your resolution. As I mentioned before your brain only has a finite amount of change willpower. If you deplete it, then you won't achieve anything. Instead make one very simple goal, which is easy to track, and achieve that first. Once you have achieved that goal, and are confident you created a new habit, then start working on another goal.

New Year's resolutions can either help you or hurt you in your habit breaking goal. You have to be extremely careful in the execution. They can be a good way to help you achieve your goals.

CHAPTER SIX

HABIT FORMING

Bad habits. Now we're going to move into a different direction. It's easier, when trying to break a bad habit, to transform it into a good habit. Not only are you eliminating something wrong, you're also forming something good. It's a win-win. Aristotle said, "We are what we repeatedly do. Excellence then is not an act, but a habit." When you were a child learning how to tie your shoes, you had to repeatedly practice over and over again before you learned how. Now you tie your shoes without even thinking. The same goes for forming a new healthy habit.

There are a lot of programs out there that say if you do something for 21 days it will be stuck in your brain. That's true to an extent. Chances are if you have successfully done your goal for 21 days in a row; you will continue to do it. But like all things, it doesn't necessarily work for everybody or every goal. Fulfilling your goal for

21 days is a huge step in the right direction as long as you remember that you still have to actively work to maintain it.

The Three R's

I spoke earlier about the three step structure of forming a habit. You can develop a new habit using that same knowledge. The three R's are; reminder, routine, reward. 'Reminder' is the trigger for your habit. Routine is the habit itself. 'Reward' is the positive thing that makes your brain want to continue to repeat the habit.

Step one is to set a reminder for your new habit. You definitely do need motivation to start a new habit, but motivation isn't enough. And it's definitely not the only way. You have to remember to do your new habit. There are several ways to remind yourself to do something. It could simply be putting your workout clothes someplace where you will see them as soon as you wake up. Set the alarm on your phone telling you to eat a healthy lunch. No matter what it is that you want to start doing, you have to remember to do it. Picking the right reminder is key, though. The best way I know to figure out when to set a reminder is to make a couple of lists. On the first list write down everything you do every day without fail. For example; brushing your teeth, eating breakfast, going to work, turn off lights, go to bed, and so on. Those are all good things you already do that can remind you to perform your new habit. Such as, after I eat breakfast, I'll go for a walk.

On the second list write down everything that happens to you every day. For example; you stop at a stop sign, you hear your favorite song, a commercial comes on, and you get a text. With both of this list you have a wide array of things that you already respond to that you can use as a reminder. If you want to start moving more, every time you hear your favorite song, dance to it. Don't do this if you're driving, though.

Step two is to create a habit that is super easy to start. There are lots of shows on TV showing people shedding lots of weight in a short amount of time. Or you see the runners or swimmers at the Olympics. It makes you want to achieve the same thing. Everybody has those moments where you think you can be just like them. The enthusiasm is great, but it's important to know that lasting changes are a product of habit. Remember, in the words of Leo Babauta, "Make it so easy that you can't say no." At first, performance doesn't matter. The only thing that matters is you strive to do something. Don't worry about how long you run, or how many veggies you eat, it just matters that you are running or eating vegetables. First, decide what you want your new habit to be. Then ask yourself, "How can I make this so easy that I can't say no?"

Step three is to create a reward. You have to celebrate. Celebration is an important part of life. You want to continue to do something that makes you feel good. Since you have to repeat an action for it to become a habit you have to find a way to reward yourself for doing it. If your goal is to exercise, then every time you finish a work out tell yourself, "Good job," or, "Today was a great day." You can also choose to say "Victory" or "Success" every time you practice the new habit. Give yourself credit no matter how big or small the success was.

Step by Step

That's an easy way to start adopting a new healthy habit. Some habits are going to be harder than others to adopt. Here are few other tips to help adopt a new habit.

Make the habit daily. New habits that you only do every few days are harder to adopt. If you want to start exercising, make sure you exercise once a day for the first 30 days. After the first 30 days, you can step down to three or four times a week.

Write down your goal. When you write out, with pen and paper, what you want your goal to be, it will make it seem more important. It makes your idea more real when you write it down.

Make it so you can't lose. Tell yourself you're running an experiment. You're running an experiment for 30 days by doing this new habit. Experiments can't fail. It makes it seem a lot less stressful. Nothing matters until after the first 30 days, and by that time you have adopted your new habit.

A big downfall of people adopting a new habit is that they doubt there self. When you first start working out you may have the thought, "I can't do this as well as they can." Whenever that thought pops into your head add, "But if I continue to work out I will get better at it." You can use this technique with anything.

Know what could happen. Be sure you know all the consequences of not starting your new habit, and know the impact of starting your new habit. Suppose your goal is eating healthier. If you don't start eating healthier, you could start gaining weight and develop health problems. If you do start eating healthier, you will lose weight and have more energy during the day.

Do it for yourself. Don't bog yourself down with the thoughts of what you should do. Instead, focus on what you want to do. You're making these changes for yourself and not for anybody else. Work towards things that motivate you and make your life better. Don't think you have to live your life like everybody around you does.

Switch Bad for Good

One of the best ways to break a bad habit is to switch it out for a good one. It helps to trick your brain and contributes to reduce cravings.

- As always, you have to first identify your triggers. You cannot break bad habits until you figure out what triggers them.

- For every trigger identify a good habit that you could do instead. Instead of smoking when you wake up, what are you going to do? Good habits could be; exercise, meditation, decluttering, organizing, and more.

- For, at least a month, be consistent with those triggers. Every time a trigger comes up act on the good habit you decided to do. The more consistent you are, the more the new habit will become ingrained, and the less you will think of the bad habit.

- Avoid severe trigger situations. You can't always switch out all triggers for new habits. As mentioned before, you might want to skip going out with friends after work for a little while. At least until you get a handle on controlling your urges.

- Discover ways to fight the strong urges. Even though the goal is to switch out the bad habit for a good habit, you will still get the urge to do the bad habit. You will likely need a backup plan when fighting urges.

- Find supportive help. Have somebody you can talk to if things get really rough. Some bad habits are tougher to break than others, and you will go through some tough times, so having somebody you can talk to will help you work through the tough times.

- Stay positive. There will be times when negative thoughts pop into your head. You will have self-sabotaging moments. But the key is to stay positive. When negative thoughts come up, remind yourself why you're doing this. Remind yourself that you're changing yourself for the better.

CHAPTER SEVEN

BE SUPPORTIVE

The human mind has the amazing ability to be able to talk you out of doing what you know is right. It can come up with crazy reasons why you shouldn't do something that you know you need to do. You want to work out, "Why? It will make you sweaty." You want to quit smoking, "You'll feel more stress if you do." You want to go to be earlier, "But then you'll miss Jimmy Kimmel." See what I mean. You have to find a way to tell your brain to shut up, and an accountability partner will help you do just that.

Growing up you probably had friends that you would vent to, and they would help you feel better about a situation. An accountability partner works much in the same way.

It will probably feel foreign or uncomfortable the first time. That's a good thing. The uncomfortable feeling is your brain resisting the change. Embrace those feelings. It will be worth it once you work through them.

The role of an accountability partner is to keep you accountable. They help as an outside force to tell your brain to shut up. Their only purpose is to keep you on track. They are there for you when you feel like straying from your path. They're there for you when you wake up in the middle of the night wanting a cupcake. Or when you are extremely stressed out, and you want a cigarette.

Your partner can be anybody that you resonate with. There is no need to pay a professional. They could be a family member, co-worker, friend, or somebody else that is trying to achieve the same goal. Find someone that you connect with and trust to hold you accountable. Be completely open about your goal. What you want to achieve and when you want to achieve it. They are there to be your cheerleader and to hold you to your commitment. Here are some things to look for in choosing your accountability partner:

1. They're reliable. They are easily reached whenever wherever.

2. They want to be your partner. You can't make somebody help you, so make sure they actually want to.

3. Make sure they can relate to you in some way. You don't want to pick someone that has never tried to lose weight to help you lose weight. They won't understand what you're going through.

4. You feel comfortable being honest and open with them, and they are comfortable giving you honest feedback.

Now that you know how to pick your accountability partner, let's talk about the benefits they will provide you. One of the biggest benefits to having an accountability partner is they will accelerate your performance. When you connect with someone one-on-one, you are able to work through the problems of your plan with them. You'll be able to make a sure fire plan to achieve your goals.

Your partner will help you measure your achievements. A good partner will help you to set milestones to reach along the way. It will be easier for you to keep track of your success, and keep you from becoming discouraged. Their outside eyes will see your success more easily than you will be able to.

They will help to validate your thoughts and ideas. Having someone to bounce your ideas off of, besides yourself, will help you to make decisions. They can give you honest outside information. They will help to silence your inner critic.

They help to keep you engaged. Things will come up that will try to distract you from your goals, and you will have someone there to help you stay the path. When you're bored, they will be there for you to talk to. Just knowing that you have somebody there for you will help you to keep your eye on the prize.

Ultimately they will hold you responsible. They are there behind you, pushing you towards your goals. They keep you from getting distracted and hold you accountable. Having a weekly check in with someone, and knowing you have to tell them what you have done this week to achieve your goal, will make you more likely to stay proactive. They keep you from making excuses, and, instead, make deliberate actions towards your end goal.

This isn't to say that you can't achieve your goals by yourself. There are people out there that can, but it takes a lot more willpower. Having a support system will make all the difference in the world.

CHAPTER EIGHT

BOOST YOUR POWER

And that's willpower. Willpower is probably one of the last things you need to work on though. If you don't know what you're trying to change, or why you're doing it, then willpower isn't going to help. You could have great willpower, but without a purpose it's going to fall flat. It's like building a house. You can have all the wood you need, but if you don't have the nails, it's not going to stay together. Once you have your plan in place, then you can move onto willpower.

Willpower and self-control are imperative building blocks for a happy and prosperous life. Some of the most persuasive evidence comes from these two studies.

The first is the marshmallow experiment. Psychologist Walter Mischel started the experiment in the 1960s. He would offer four-year-olds a choice of a marshmallow now or two marshmallows if they could wait 15 minutes. He and his associates then tracked those students as they grew up. They found that the children who were willing to wait 15 minutes for the marshmallows achieved greater academic success, better health, and a less likely chance of divorce.

In the second study, 1,000 children were studied from birth to 32. Researchers found that the children's self-control could predict the future of their health, substance dependence, criminal offenses, and personal finances. It was even true when they eliminated factors such as intelligence and social class.

Use it or lose it

Everybody knows these two factors about muscles:

- Muscles get stronger when exercised

- Muscles can be overworked, which leaves them weak until they have time to rest

But here are some interesting things you may not know.

- In a study, some participants were told not to think about a white bear. Thought-suppression takes a good deal of self-control, especially when told not to think about something. After that, they were told to limit their intake of beer during a taste test because there would be a driving test later. The thought-suppression participants drank more than the non-thought-suppression participants.

- In another study, participants that were asked to suppress their emotions during an upsetting movie gave up sooner during a physical stamina test than those who were freely allowed to express their emotions.

- In a third study, women watched a documentary while seated near a candy bowl. In some, the candy bowl was right next to the woman, in others the candy bowl was across the room from them. Later, they were given hard puzzles to solve. Those that had been seated close to the candy bowl gave up sooner than those who weren't.

In each of these studies, the people that were forced to overuse their willpower or self-control could not fully finish subsequent tasks. Their willpower had been depleted. Now let's look at some ways to strengthen your willpower.

1. Don't keep your willpower depleted

If you have plans to help your friend move heavy pieces of furniture, you're not going to spend 30 minutes before lifting weights. You know your energy will be depleted before you help your friend. The same goes for your willpower. Exercising self-control is an excellent way to build willpower, never giving yourself a break is a good way to deplete it.

2. Meditation

Meditation seems to come up a lot when looking for ways to change habits. It is a great way to strengthen your ability to control your thoughts. But what is meditation? Meditation is simply the practice of bringing your thoughts to the present moment. 47% of lives are spent either thinking about the past, or what has to be done in the future. Leaving us with very little time to think about what we are doing at this present moment. Our brains are very undisciplined. They like to wander. With 10 minutes of meditation each day it will help strengthen your mind and help keep it from wandering. Studies have shown after just 2 to 3 days of 10-minute meditation your brain will be able to focus better, you will have more energy and a lot less stress.

3. Use your imagination

Imagination is an amazing way to improve willpower. The body can respond the same way to an imaginary scenario as the real one. If you imagine laying on a beach, listening to the waves crash, your body will respond by relaxing. On the other hand, if you think about going to work and having a meeting with your boss, your body will tense in response. Dieters are in a constant state of depletion. As a result, they feel everything more intensely. Imagination is able to help control these irritations

In a study, participants were asked to watch a movie with a bowl of chocolate placed nearby. One group was told to imagine they had decided to eat as much as they want. The second group was told to imagine they had eaten none. The third group was told to imagine they had decided to eat the chocolate later. The first group ate more than the other two. Then when given the opportunity to eat later, those that had imagined they would eat later, ate less than the others. They even reported a lesser desire to consume the candy.

4. Use your opposite hand

Researchers have conducted studies that tested corrective actions. One they found that worked particularly well was to use your opposite hand. Your brain is wired to use your dominant hand so it will take willpower to use the non-dominate hand. To practice this, choose a time during the day to use your non-dominate hand. I would suggest doing no more than an hour at a time. More than an hour may deplete your willpower

5. Distract yourself

It's even possible to use your imagination to distract yourself from unwanted thoughts. Just like in the study mentioned earlier about the white bear. When you tell yourself not to think about something, it's going to continually pop back into your head. Train yourself to think about something else. If you don't want to think about that white bear, or cigarettes, or candy, flip your thoughts to something else. Instead of a white bear, think of a black bear. Instead of cigarettes, think of chewing gum. Instead of candy, think of fruit. That puts you in complete control of your thoughts

6. Control your stress

I have mentioned stress several times throughout this book. Stress is the main culprit of many problems. When you become stressed, you'll tend to fall back into old habits. Most of the time you won't even realize it because your body goes into autopilot. When you're stressed, your body releases stress hormones, mainly cortisol.

Cortisol increases your cravings for carbohydrates. Carbs will lower your cortisol levels. Which is probably perhaps why you turn to your friends Ben and Jerry. Alcohol is also a depressant that reduces your cortisol levels. Both of those options hold some negative side effect and aren't helping you to kick those bad habits.

Fortunately, we know these things so you can have control over what you do. The stress response is the same as the fight or flight response, so anything that counterattacks that response will do. Start responding to those stressors by listening to calming music, visualizing calming scenes, or moderate exercise. Whatever works for you. Researchers also say viewing funny videos can help counteract willpower depletion.

The more you practice these habits, the more likely they will be there to help you when major stressors arise.

7. A step at a time

Most of the time people give up on goals, not because of the lack of willpower, but because of feeling overwhelmed in what they are trying to accomplish. I have mentioned something similar to this before. Break your goals down into manageable pieces. That way you can see each step you take instead of trying to consume the whole thing. This also keeps you from depleting your willpower, keeping you recharged and ready to continue working at all times.

8. Be yourself

It takes a lot of effort to suppress you typical behaviors, personality, and preferences. Not surprisingly, it also depletes willpower. Psychologist Mark Muraven found that people who exert self-control to make others happy were more easily depleted than individuals who held true to their own goals and happiness. People pleasures may find they are at a disadvantage when it comes to willpower as opposed to those who are secure and comfortable with their self.

9. Change your speech

In another correction study, researchers conducted to modify the subject's natural speech. This would include resisting the urge to say a cuss word, or simply change from saying "hey" to "hello." It takes willpower to make the conscious effort to change one's speech, especially when we typically speak out of instinct. It doesn't matter what you do to change your speech, as long as you make a conscious effort to switch things up. Just like using your opposite hand, choose a chunk of your day where you will change the way you speak. You also need to decide what it is that you are going to change. You might choose to stop swearing, or to stop saying slang words like "ain't." Remember to only practice this for about an hour at a time, or you may deplete your willpower. After only two weeks you will see an increase in your willpower.

10. Keep temptations at bay

With most habits, you have a weakness for what you like to consume. If you drink too much keep alcohol out of your house. If you smoke, get rid of all your cigarettes. If you snack a lot, either get rid of the junk food or put it out of sight. There will be times when you see your weakness, and you will need to make a plan for that moment. Decide how you are going to handle it. If your weakness is junk food and you have children, chances are junk food is going to enter your house at some point. No matter where the kids got the food, grandma, trick or treating, school, work out a plan where you don't constantly see it. Work with your spouse or significant other. Have them take all the junk food and put it where you don't know where it is. If the kids want some, they have to ask the other parent, not you. And you have to promise that you won't beg and plead to know where it is. That takes a little willpower in itself, but a lot less than trying to keep from eating the junk food that you see.

Willpower is just like any other muscle in your body. With the right practice, it can be strengthened. I have just given you 10 ways to increase your willpower and self-control, but don't try to do all 10 at once. You'll just end up driving yourself crazy. Think of training your willpower just like you would prepare for a race. On your first day of training, you're not going to run the full 26 miles. Not unless you're already an Olympic runner. Instead, you will increase the amount you run every day. Choose one of these to start using on a daily basis. Once you feel that's not working for you anymore, pick a different one. Before you know it, you will be more mentally strong.

CHAPTER NINE

MEDITATIVE STATE

Mediation has proved to be very helpful in most aspects of life. It has shown up numerous times already in this book. Since it seems to be so useful, I figured I would dedicate a whole chapter to it. We'll take a deeper look into the benefits of meditation and how it will help you break your bad habits. Then I will give you a simple step by step on how to get started meditating for beginners. If you already meditate, then you have a leg up.

Ask anybody that meditates, and they will tell you it's good for you. But in what way? Is that just from years of practice, or is there scientific research out there that proves it's good for you? Here are some general ways that mediation can help:

- Improves willpower

- Improves focus

- Decreases stress

- Improves ability to learn

- Increases energy

There are over 3,000 scientific studies that examine the benefits of meditation. I'm going to summarize some of the findings for you.

- Decreases depression

In Belgium, a study was conducted at five middle schools involving approximately 400 students. Professor Filip Raes concluded that the students that participated in mindfulness meditation reduced indication of anxiety, stress, and depression for up to six months later. At the University of California, a similar study was conducted with formerly depressive patients and concluded that mindfulness meditation reduced ruminative thinking and dysfunctional beliefs.

- Reduces panic disorder

The American Journal of Psychiatry published a study where 22 patients diagnosed with panic disorder were submitted to 3 months of meditation and relaxation training. 20 of the 22 participants showed that their panic and anxiety had been reduced significantly, and the changes were maintained at follow-up.

- Increases concentration

Harvard neuroscientists ran an experiment where 16 people took part in an 8-week mindfulness course. They used guided meditation and integration of mindfulness in everyday activities. Sara Lazer, Ph.D., reported at the end, MRI scans showed that gray matter concentration increased in areas of the brain involved in learning, memory, emotion regulation, sense of self, and perspective.

- Increases focus in spite of distraction

Emory University did a study that demonstrated that participants with more mediation experience exhibited increased connectivity within the brain controlling attention. The neural relationships may be involved in the development of cognitive skills.

- Prevents you from falling in a multitasking trap

Multitasking is a dangerous productivity myth that will deplete you of energy and is a source of stress. Switching between tasks is costly to your brain which can cause feelings of distraction and dissatisfaction. In a study conducted by the University of Washington and the University of Arizona, human resources personnel took part in 8 weeks of in either mindfulness meditation or body relaxation techniques. They were given stressful multitasking tests before and after training. Groups that had practice meditation showed lower stress levels and a better recall of the tasks they had done. They also switched between tasks less often, concentrating on one task for a longer amount of time.

- Increases unconscious mind awareness

A study done by the University of Sussex found that people who practiced mindfulness meditation experienced a longer paused between unconscious impulses and action. They were also less susceptible to hypnosis.

- Reduces heart diseases and stroke

Cardiovascular disease kills more people in the world than anything else. A study performed in 2012, studied 200 high-risk individuals. They were asked to, either, take part in a health education class promoting better diet and exercise, or take a class on transcendental meditation. During the next five years, they found that those who took the meditation class decreased their overall risk of heart disease, stroke, and death by 48%.

- Increases compassion and decreases worry

After 9 weeks of compassion cultivation training, participants showed significant improvement in all three domains of compassion (compassion for others, receiving compassion, and self-compassion).

- Decreases emotional eating

Scientists have found that transcendental meditation decreases the likelihood of emotional eating, which helps to prevent obesity.

There is a lot more scientific information out there that proves meditation can help with all aspects of life. It's no wonder that it shows up a lot in contributing to quit bad habits.

Simple meditation practice

If you've never meditated before, I would suggest doing a guided meditation. A quick search on the internet will turn up several apps and downloads for guided meditation. Some free choices are Omvana, Headspace, Calm, Smiling Mind, and Take a Break.

If you want to meditate on your own here is a simple meditation practice designed by Headspace App founder, Andy Puddicombe:

1. Find a quiet room where you can sit comfortably upright with no distraction.

2. Set a 10-minute timer, and get comfortable in your chair.

3. Find something in your line of vision to focus on for 6 deep breaths. With each exhale, allow your body to soften as you become more relaxed. On the 6th exhale, close your eyes.

4. Focus your attention on the points of contact between your body and the chair and floor. Notice the sensation of your arms, back, and bottom on the chair, and your feet on the floor.

5. Then become aware of your surroundings. Notice all the sounds and smells around you. Anything that you can sense without your sight.

6. Then focus on your breath. Notice how your chest expands when you breathe in and how it contracts when you exhale.

7. Once you're comfortable with the rhythm of your breathing, begin to count. 1 on the inhale, 2 on the exhale, all the way up to 10. This will keep your mind focused on your breath and keep it from wandering.

8. When you make it to 10, start back over at 1. Do not count 11, 12, 13, etc.

9. While you breathe, allow your thoughts to come and go. You can't stop yourself from thinking. What you want to do is avoid lingering on one thought. The moment you realize your mind has wandered, bring it back to your breaths.

10. Continue until your timer goes off.

The first time you do this, it will probably seem awkward and weird. It's just like adopting a new habit. The more you do it, the less uncomfortable it becomes, and the easier it will be to do.

Here are some other, more advanced, mediation options:

- Candle starting

If you have problems focusing, you can light a candle and stare at it. Make sure the candle is at eye level. If you find your mind wandering, return your focus to what the flame is doing. Another level up is to stare at the candle without blinking. It will eventually make you cry which refreshes your eyes.

- Mantra

The repetition of words helps you to find calm and focus. You can find different mantras online, or you can make up your own. It doesn't matter what you say as long as it resonates with you, and you're happy with it.

- Visualization

Another fun and easy way to meditate is to visualize an idyllic being or setting in your mind. You can make it whatever you want. Embellishing it as much or as little as you need.

- Become the Observer

Become the observer of your mind. Close your eyes and focus on the spot, about an inch, above the spot between your eyebrows, third eye chakra. Begin to focus on what you mind and body is feeling, thinking and doing.

You should now be able to use meditation to help you break your bad habits, and, in the process, start a new good, habit.

I'm sure you are dying to start working on getting rid of that bad habit that's been bothering you, so I'll wrap this up. Remember to keep this simple. Don't overwhelm yourself with too many goals, or trying too many of these techniques at once. Be prepared to fail and meet naysayers, they are inevitable, but you don't have to let them control you. If nothing else, please remember you deserve to live the best life possible.

PART V

Chapter 1: Who are you talking to?

For our purposes, a conversation is an exchange of verbally communicated ideas between two people. One of them is you, and the other is someone else. What is the degree of familiarity? Is it someone you've known all your life or is it that new co-worker that has been in the office for only a week? The relationship between those in the conversation helps establish a logical starting point.

An exchange between people who have only known each other professionally usually begins more formally than talk between two people who only know each other outside of their professional lives. It's appropriate to have 'small talk' precede the main focus in professional conversations due to the fact that people don't interact as often when this is the nature of the relationship and there are more uncertainties about one another.

With respect to personal relationships, there is a difference between what we shall call simple relationships and invested relationships. Because relationships have the potential to evolve, connections might be transitioning from simple to a more complex relationship such as that of a someone we've started to date or perhaps a new mother-in-law. In instances of changing connections, the capital and the stakes of conversations usually increase in value.

Certainly there are instances where two people are connected both personally and professionally, sometimes for a long period of time. Playing golf with business partners is a scenario that could lead to such a situation. This can be a little complicated, and one or both may tend to suspend the rules of engagement due to familiarity. This may require backing up and trying to have more formally constructed conversation.

If the person you're conversing with is someone new to you, it's really important to know yourself well and be aware of any personal tendencies or personality traits that might be perceived as 'a bit much' until others get to know you. Most of us can think of a personality quirk for just about anybody we know, including ourselves. Others who know us well have likely offered constructive criticism of the more challenging aspects of our personality and we should take this to heart.

Chapter 2: What are your motivations?

Any conversation has a purpose. Perhaps it is simply to maintain good relations in an established friendship. We engage in many conversations with no real purpose or objective in mind other than to maintain connection a light-hearted connection – as in the one we have perhaps with someone who we encounter once a week or so that works the check-out line in the grocery store.

Conversations don't always have a destination to be reached or some other tangible outcome, depending upon the nature of the relationship. Simple relationships such as with someone working the check-out line with who we might have a brief conversation in passing are quite different from more invested relationships, such as that with a romantic companion, relative, or professional colleague. Our motivations for engagement vary here and we need to have at least a small appreciation for the purpose, lest we lose track of what we might have invested.

Romantic and business conversations, different as they may be in terms of topics, tone, and other attributes of communication do have in common that we are talking about some level of investment on our part and presumably on the part of someone else as well. Whether it's someone we're thinking about proposing marriage or a merger, there's a lot of investment in either case.

All invested conversations require that the wants, needs, and demands of one person be measured alongside those of the other. Are you asking someone to help your business grow by offering an innovative analysis of sales data? Are you persuading your spouse that it's time for the family to grow with the addition of another child? An inventory will need to be taken in either scenario of the points that are shared in addition to where there are differences. Unless something goes terribly wrong and invested relationships dissolve, conversations will continue to occur and should reflect an effort on the part of two people to recall and maintain an awareness of what they are asking of each other.

Chapter 3: How will you prepare?

When a meeting is scheduled or a date is on the calendar, there is often much anticipation about how things will go. Anticipation leads to expectation or in some cases, reservation. Going over the possible outcomes in your mind followed up by a rehearsal or mock conversation is a good way to cover your bases and provide a sense of confidence about the impending conversation. If someone else is not available, read a dialogue with several exchanges as means to warm up before the actual conversation takes place

A number of variables can come into play that would affect preparation. A lot depends on whether the conversation taking place is between people in a new versus existing relationship. If the other person is new to you, other than being resourceful and gleaning some pertinent facts for conversation fodder, about all you can do is have some topics in mind in the event that the conversation stalls.

If you have the benefit of having past conversations with someone, this is helpful in that you can recall how that person tends to engage with you. Will they lead the conversation if you give them the chance or will they defer? In the cases where there is familiarity, more preparation will have to be put into a conversation that is anticipated to be strained. For instance, if conflict resolution is a likely aspect, think of appropriate questions ahead of time and ways to address issues that diffuse tension, and create a more relaxed environment. Think about acknowledging differences up front using a reconciliatory tone.

Chapter 4: Which tactics are indispensable?

So we're at the point where introductions and small talk are over. From start to end, there are multiple tactics than can be employed to enhance the outcome, much like playing a hand of cards in a timely fashion.

Starting a conversation in amicable fashion is critical. Cut the small talk short or eliminate it if the other person is short on time or simply prefers to get down to business in short order. If it is your first conversation with someone, be mindful that you never get a second chance to make a first impression, and that impression, be it fair or not, may be formed very quickly. Early on acknowledge the other party's interests or concerns prior to stating your own, if you are the one to open things up or lead the conversation.

From start to finish, be constantly mindful and feel things out on everything from the tone of the conversation to how the other person is reacting. If a conversation gets out of hand or veers off course very far, it may be difficult to achieve the original goals that were set out. Quietly ask yourself "is everything going well, or should I try to make an adjustment?" If the other person stumbles or seems confused about how things are proceeding, try to improve clarity so that both of you are confident about how things are going relative to what might have been anticipated.

Being perceived as focused and giving the other person your full attention is perhaps the most important characteristic of someone who has productive conversations. If you come across as aloof or distracted it will probably be a downer. Someone may have taken a significant chunk of time out of their day to set aside for what they thought was going to be a meaningful exchange and instead they are totally deflated by someone who seems somewhere else.

We have already shed light on coming up with appropriate questions in advance for what are anticipated to be challenging conversations. This is particularly true if modern electronic communication or social media exchanges have preceded or led to the conversation. Incomplete thoughts or confusion created by these shorthand approaches to communicating may result in questions that should be dealt with at the beginning of the conversation. Heck, they may be the entire reason for the conversation. Giving prior thought to appropriate questions is good in any case as the most relevant questions may not come to mind if you wait until the conversation has begun. It is likely that the most curious questions, which reflect serious thought on your part, will come up in advance. Modify questions if you perhaps initially asked something too broad.

Maintain composure rather than get defensive when someone is confrontational or insulting. Disarming someone with a witty or playful response give you the control that they forfeited by deploying counterproductive language.

Give thorough responses that indicate you have respect for other peoples' questions. Abbreviated or literal responses in addition to being insufficiently clear, may also suggest a lack of respect or consideration for what the other person is trying to learn. If their facial expression or other observable response suggests that they did not get the information they were wanting, politely ask them to clarify what they were asking for if it is not abundantly clear.

Be mindful of where the conversation is going and be ready to get it back on track if it is headed into unproductive or counterproductive turf. Be prepared to usurp the role of leading the conversation should it stall. The other person might not be inclined to take the initiative here, and you may have no way of knowing if they're new to you.

Just like you shouldn't give a literal or abbreviated response, you shouldn't ask questions that would lead someone to think you were asking for such. Questions that demand responses beyond the mundane will give the other person a chance to share a more detailed account leaving them feeling as though they got to share the whole story.

People want to be recognized and given due credit. Do yourself a favor and take the opportunity in advance. If they feel the need to bring attention to an accomplishment before you mention it, they are indicating that they feel a lack of respect. Recognition will make future conversations more productive because validation will motivate people to be more engaged.

We need to listen effectively in order to gain the respect of those we engage in conversation. Constantly cutting them off or interrupting them will make it seem as we are dismissing their importance in the relationship. One is not listening effectively if they are unable to stay in the present moment. Diverting the conversation may also be regarded as not respecting someone's concern about the topic at hand.

Making demands or requests in a conversation is a sensitive matter. Be fair and don't ask for too much. Don't ask for something if it is going to be obvious that you haven't done anything to help yourself and just want to place a burden on the other person. No one wants to feel as though they're being taken advantage of, so consider carefully as to whether you should make a request of them.

Demonstrate that you are in the moment by actions that are visibly obvious. Record notes during the conversation or commitments you have made. Place a future date on your phone calendar when an event is mentioned. This implies intent on your part to follow through and makes the other person feel as though they've gotten something across to you and that their input was worthwhile.

Chapter 5: The Supreme Tactic – The Follow-Up Conversation

After a conversation, you must take inventory of how things went. If you know of strategic mistakes that were made along the way, make note of them and take care not to commit them in future conversations. You must hold yourself responsible for being able to recall any specific outcomes and good note-taking is the best way to accomplish this. If a conversation ends with both parties knowing what was specifically agreed to or are certain of specific commitments that were made and how outcomes are to be achieved, it may not be necessary to revisit the conversation down the road. When outcomes aren't certain and nothing was specifically agreed upon, it may be in the best interest of two people to come back together and express their views about what each took from the conversation. Revisit the points of agreement and disagreement with emphasis given as to why sentiments differed on particular subjects that were discussed. An apologetic tone might be called for if you lost your composure or you felt deficient in attention or focus. Remember that follow-up conversation may be used as a polite gesture to offer thanks or appreciation, in which case they needn't be extended affairs. If a follow-up is something of an in-between linking two major conversations, it may require more input as it establishes what will be discussed in the latter conversation.

PART VI

Chapter 1: How Technology Has Affected Our Communication Skills

Before we dive into the practical strategies of overcoming those dreaded awkward moments, there is some basic information that you should know. You see, it is my belief that seeing a full picture of the context will help you to understand the basis of your communication block better.

In truth, the world we live in today is a lot different than it used to be back in the days of covered wagons and community bathing. Yuck! It is certainly better in a myriad of ways. We have the technology, fast cars, airplanes, hell even indoor plumbing! But. Just but. It isn't better in some respects.

We Were Set Up To Fail

You see, people call this the age of communication. People call this the golden era of instant connectivity based on the ease in which we can talk to people hundreds or even thousands of miles away from us. That is certainly a great thing in all but wait. What about the people that are sitting right next to us? How connected to them are we?

Over seventy percent of the world's population admits to having a problem with communicating properly with people in their families. Think about that for a moment. SEVENTY PERCENT! That is just mind boggling. And to put things into perspective, more than three out of four of your neighbors probably face this same issue as you do.

It is also faithful to a vast extent that a consequence of that problem leads to one not having the proper communication skills to engage on a personal level with strangers or primary acquaintances.

Have you noticed that in the past, before telephones were in every household, it was so much easier to talk to people face to face? That is because for the longest time, excluding the post that came every week or the occasional messenger pigeon that often took days to reach a destination seventy miles away, it was the **only** form of communication with someone! If you wanted to have a full conversation in real time with someone you knew that wasn't living in your own home you had to move your butt up from your seat, walk over to their house, knock on their door, open your mouth, and talk to them. Sounds harsh eh? Now think how many people do that now in the modern age.

This meant that communication was futile to survival in the past. If you needed something from someone, you had to physically and verbally ask for it. This also meant that you would have to communicate regularly with everyone around you to get stuff done.

Past Customs Allowed For Natural Conversations

In the past, it was customary to greet everyone with a smile when you're walking down the street. Not doing so was considered bad manners. In contrast, people living in the modern age are so glued to their smartphones or listening to their music with earphones shoved deep down their ear drums that their mouths don't even move much anymore. People are LESS connected to one another today.

In the past humans had to interact by speaking several times a day and as a result, people were not only more friendly to one another, they became more fluent and natural at talking and communicating with their peers. They had proper training on a daily basis just by opening their mouths more often. How easy is that?

We Were Not Given The Chance To Develop Our Social Skills

You see, children in days gone by were taught from a young age how to socialize. They were sent outside to make their friends, and they were taught how to be self-sufficient. This gave them the confidence to speak to others. In school, they were instructed on what appropriate conversation was. Children were often taught not to speak unless spoken to. This was to teach them to listen to those around them truly and to respond in a meaningful and understanding way. This training not only made them good listeners but also compassionate adults that were able to hold productive conversations in the highest of social settings. As you can see, a conversation was key to survival.

Where's The Social Gathering In The Modern Age?

Let's face it. We are all glued to our smartphones, tablets, and computers. Swiping left on Tinder, surfing the net, texting people on Facebook or iMessage. When have we ever had a decent conversation or a happy get-together with our closest friends? The truth is that we were crippled by our devices the day we got them. It is unfortunate now, isn't it?

Consequences Of Rapid Development

The hectic life and "connectivity" today has turned our society a complete one hundred and eighty degrees. We have started to take for granted the most straightforward and efficient tools for communication and replaced them with devices that we THINK are doing a better job for us. In reality people today are more closed off than they ever were and that is unfortunate. Modernization and technology have robbed us of our most core competencies, and we need to claim it back!

The Intricate Things We ARE Deprived Of:

- The gatherings with friends and family

- The lack of fun festivities

- The missing social events

- The community spirit and comradery with our peers.

- The treatment of everyone around you with respect and dignity that you wish you received.

- The Communication with our neighbors.

Possible Causes

There are many possible reasons for this silence struck pandemic. Most of it can be attributed to one or more of the many technological advances that we have seen over the years. No one person has been able to pinpoint exactly what it is that has changed the friendly ways of the world. Here are some of the possible causes. You can try to decide for yourself what you think has been the downfall of communication.

1. **The Telephone**: The invention of the phone made it easier to take the human element out of a conversation. Instead of going to someone's house every so often and staying a few hours, and having a meal, they could call to say what needed to be said, and then cut the conversation short with the excuse that they were wracking up too many minutes that month. They didn't have to stay on the phone yacking for hours on end because the person on the other end of the line agreed and hung up as well.

The telephone, back when it was invented, was so expensive that only the rich people and government agencies owned them. Created in 1876 by Alexander Graham-Bell, it was the most technologically advanced thing since the dawn of electricity. In the beginning, it cost over a thousand dollars to own a single phone. To make a call, Bell Telephone Industries charged a dollar a minute to dispatch that call. That was a lot of money considering the average worker was lucky to make fifty cents an hour. One minute call time would have been two hours wages, so most average salary households did not have a telephone in the house. That was until the early 1900's after Henry Ford invented the concept of mass production. A company made a telephone that was way cheaper than Bell Industries old phone design, and they found a better way to dispatch calls to make the calls cheaper. During this time, wages went up a lot as well. By this period the minimum wage was about two dollars an hour. This made phones more common in average households. By the nineteen seventies, a home phone was a staple in each house and calls only cost ten cents a minute. This was a great thing, as, by this time, wages were up to seven dollars an hour for minimum wage. The company that was instrumental in lowering the price of the phone? Well, these days it's known as AT&T.

Due to its cost, the telephone may not have been the downfall of modern communication, but it definitely could have had a hand in it. Particularly as it became easier, and cheaper to purchase. People called rather than stopped by, and these calls did not have to drone on and on, as time was money. This allowed conversations to become shorter, and it made its way into everyday life as well.

2. **Television:** The television was a lot cheaper than the telephone was. It was also a way to get the news a lot easier, as you didn't have to wait until a friend heard something and get back to you. There were also some good programs to watch during the day that entertained people. This entertainment made them want to stay inside and watch it all day. Well, the adults at least. Children were still sent outside to play.

The original television was black and white and only had three channels. It was small and could sit on the dining room table. Brand new, they cost about three hundred dollars, and they had long rabbit ear antennas. In the beginning, this was the only option you had, but as time went on, there were bigger console televisions available. Eventually, the color television was introduced, and some time after that, more channels were added, as cable became a thing. More and more time was spent inside watching TV. Not just by adults anymore, either.

Children were inside more often and watched shows that were geared towards their age groups. People went out and mingled with their neighbors less and less.

Television alone probably was not the downfall of the communication era, but it was a precedent to it. A lot of people began staying inside to watch their soaps instead of going outside to spend time with actual people. For the longest time, children were still sent out to play while the parents watched TV, but as the parents moved to colored cable, the children got the still working black and white rabbit-eared television, and the trend progressed as in the older days, television sets lasted forever.

3. **Game Consoles:** Today there are several hi-tech game consoles out there for people to choose from, and they are often played for hours on end, while the player ignores the outside world. Back when they were first invented, they were a lot different, but no less desirable. They were the envy of every household, and a child that had one was instantly familiar, but he never used that popularity because he was too busy inside playing his new game. When the original Atari came out, it was the sensation that swept the nation.

The first ever game console was nothing like the ones we have today. They took a lot more effort to play. To make a single move, you had to write a program first. This was difficult, but the kids in those days didn't mind, as to them it was a game console, and that was the coolest thing they had ever seen. They also learned about computer programming before home computers were a thing. As time progressed, the programs were written into the game at production, so all kids had to do was play the game. They also went from almost fifteen hundred dollars to a hundred and fifty dollars. While that was still pretty expensive, it was a lot more affordable than the Atari. The most popular and innovative of these new consoles? The Nintendo Entertainment System, or NES for short. It was the console that every kid wanted, and most kids were able to get for Christmas or their birthday. With the debut of the game Super Mario Brothers stepping away from the typical games of Pong and Galactica, this thrilling console had kids of all ages, and even adults gathered around it to enjoy it. This further engulfed them into their anti-social bubbles as they were too engrossed in the games to go outside.

Video Games are blamed by many as being the downfall of modern society. That can be seen as accurate, as there were so many people beginning to stay indoors rather than going outside. However, there were plenty of friendly people left in the world, and people still visited one another, so is this the truth? Maybe as they progressed, but it was not an immediate destruction.

4. **Media:** This one can be brutal. People are so easily influenced by the media, that they could tell the people that Donald Trump farted unicorns, and they would almost believe it. Okay, maybe not that sorry, but that is the general idea with the media. Nowadays, the media is filled with bombings, kidnappings and

other fear mongering materials that it makes it hard to trust the people around you.

In the beginning, the news just stated that. The news. It gave news of the war if there was one, and news With all the fear-inducing news, it makes it hard to want to even talk to anyone, because it seems as if everyone is a murderer now. This is not a conducive environment like friendly ways of the past.

Media could be considered the downfall of the friendly atmosphere, as it seeds fear of the human race in your mind, and that is what seems to have closed people off from their natural chatty instincts.

5. **Internet:** The dawn of the web saw a rise in introverts massively. It is no secret that the web has taken over the minds of most of our youth. This goes hand in hand with the media, as it is the primary source of all media output.

So those are some of the possible causes of why it is harder now to talk to people than it used to be. Of course, for some people, it is more difficult than others. Individuals with anxiety or shyness have a hard time even talking to people that are deemed safe by people they trust. It isn't caused by fear, just a nervousness that causes these people to clam up. Chances are since you are reading this, you are one of these people.

Do not fret. This book will help you get through this. However, be prepared. Sometimes it takes more than self-help, and if your problem has deeper seated issues, you may want to get the help of a psychiatrist. If these tips do not help, it is best to seek the help of one if you wish to be more of a conversationalist, and it is essential for your mental and emotional health. There will be more on that at the end of this book.

Chapter 2: Conversation Tips

Step One-Talking to Yourself

This may seem a little silly, but it does help. It is the easiest way to get over your shyness, as it is more awkward to talk to yourself than it is to talk to other people. You just have to get past the first hump of not wanting to look like a fool and own it.

Go into a room with a mirror, start by offering your hand to shake and mime shaking hands with the person staring back at you while introducing yourself. This may feel a little weird, as there is not going to be a meeting of hands, due to you only having the conversation with yourself.

Once you get past the standard greeting, it is time to hold a conversation. You can either say your mirrored self's responses, or you can keep them in your head. This is where it can get tricky. You cannot think of specific to you answers, rather, you have to think of general answers, as you are not the person you are talking to. Talk away as if an actual person was holding a conversation with you. You can think of this as a live diary, but more civilized and social, as you don't want to spill your secrets to someone who is mostly standing in as a stranger.

Here is a little scenario to help you visualize what it would be like.

SCENARIO

Kelly had just finished reading *How to Talk to Anyone: Ten Secrets You Wish You Knew*, and she wanted to try out the first tip, which was called "Talking to Yourself." She stepped into her bathroom and closed the door.

"Okay, Kelly. You can do this. You have to become better at holding a conversation, as your husband's job requires you to attend various social events with him."

Looking into the mirror she offered her hand to the cold glass, feeling slightly foolish.

"Hello, my name is Kelly. And you are?"

In her head, she planned the response.

I am Richard Simms. A pleasure to meet you, Kelly. She used her husband's boss's name as that was the one she was sure she knew.

"Pleasure to meet you too, sir. How are you and your wife and kids?"

They are doing well, as am I. How about your children?

"Oh, no children yet sir. Wanting to get ahead financially first."

A great plan, I must say. Children are very expensive little buggers.

Kelly was interrupted then, as her husband walked into the bathroom.

"Who on Earth are you talking to?"

"I am practicing holding a conversation. I don't want to embarrass you tomorrow at the banquet." Kelly blushed.

"Awe, sweetheart, you could never embarrass me, but I appreciate the effort, and I am glad you are taking the steps necessary to better yourself. I am proud of you." Her husband kissed her forehead and left.

After that boost of confidence, Kelly found it much easier to practice her conversation skills and felt less awkward about talking to herself in the mirror.

It may seem embarrassing to talk to yourself in a mirror, but after awhile it will be much easier, as you will start to feel better about helping yourself become the best that you can be. If someone comes in and asks you what you are doing, explain to them what you are trying to do. You never know, maybe they will try it for themselves.

Of course, there is still a stigma that talking to yourself means that you are crazy, but once you explain that you are not trying to be weird, you just are trying to become better at conversation, people will understand. It is getting harder and harder for people to hold a normal conversation in this world, so it is always refreshing to hear that someone is trying to better themselves.

Step Two- Have a Few Ice Breakers

It is no secret that after the initial introductions conversation gets awkward if there are no real conversation starters in the room. You say hello, state your name, and ask a few questions about what the person does, and how their day has been, but after that is over, this is when the conversation dies out with a bunch of "Ums" and "Uhhh." Having a few icebreakers is always important as you can keep the conversation going, and often have a few laughs going at the end.

Of course, it is hard to tell exactly what you should use as an icebreaker, and that is why most people have a hard time keeping the conversation going. However, few foolproof icebreakers will make talking to

someone a breeze. This section will go over some ice breakers to use...
and some to avoid.

Real Ice Breakers

1. **Latest viral cat video:** Pretty much everyone in the world loves
cat videos, and a lot of people have seen them. Bringing that up
in conversation is always a good way of push conversation
along. It is a safe topic that won't offend people, and if
someone hasn't seen the video, you can show it to them,
eliciting a few laughs and smiles. Almost everyone loves cat
videos.

2. **Food:** Everyone eats. So ask the person what kind of food they
like. It is always pertinent to ask them first because if they are
vegan, you don't want to say "Bacon is the greatest, is it not?"
Discuss different cuisines, and if they have not tried one of your
favorites, suggest a good place find it. Talking about food can
bring people closer together, as they find common likes and
interests in cuisines.

3. **Music:** Everyone listens to music. No matter what their tastes,
everyone loves music. You cannot deny the fact that life would
be boring without it. It fills the awkward silences, and it can
bring up someone who is down. There is no escaping the fact
that music is tied to emotions as well. Try asking the person
what their favorite song is. Ask them the genres they like. If you
find you have some interests that are similar, that is great, and
that will further boost the conversation.

4. **Hobbies:** Everyone has a passion that probably has nothing to do with their job. Hobbies are what make life interesting. It is a safe topic to approach because many people love to talk about what they enjoy, but rarely anyone asks.

5. **Anything to do with interests:** Pretty much anything to do with personal interests is safe to talk about because people love to talk about themselves. They like to make known what they enjoy, and they love when someone shows interest in them. However, most people are too shy to talk about themselves unprompted because they do not wish to seem conceited.

Bad Ice Breakers

1. **Politics:** There are so many different opinions out there, and unfortunately with the policy, everyone thinks that they are right. The conversation can get awkward if you are a Democrat butting heads with a Republican. That is only the tip of the iceberg though. Tempers often flare at the slightest mention that either party may be corrupt, so it is best all around to just avoid the conversation entirely.

2. **Religion:** This is another one that is best avoided. Religion is a very sensitive subject for some, and no one wants someone else's religion shoved in their faces. That is why you are better off keeping this one put away.

3. **Life choices:** It is great that you have decided to become a vegan and all, but you do not have to convert everyone who is around you. Same with any of the life choices you make, whether you sell Avon or those scammy weight loss products,

virtually no one wants to hear the spiel. Save it for if you are asked.

So there you have it. Some good and some not-so-good icebreakers to help you extend any conversation past the initial hell0. Once you can establish a gateway to the conversation, you will be able to carry on a lot easier than you would if you had not used an icebreaker at all, and were floundering about like a fish out of water, trying to figure out what to say.

How These Tips Help

These tips help you relax a little bit. They give you a little confidence boost, knowing that you are prepared to hold a conversation with people you may meet because you have practiced the basics. It is a lot easier to do something once you have practiced it a few times.

It also helps you get past the awkwardness, as nothing is more awkward than holding a conversation with yourself. You will be able to talk to someone without feeling silly because you couldn't possibly feel any goofier than you did speak to a mirror.

Follow these tips to get the ball rolling on talking to people.

Chapter 3: Holding a Conversation

Now that you have gotten past the tips on how to approach and talk to someone, it is time to move on to the advice on how to hold a conversation. This is important because starting a conversation is only a small part of the battle. This means that you have to be able to continue a conversation past the point of the icebreaker.

Conversations do not have to be hours long, but you do have to keep them at a length that does not make you seem rude, or disinterested. If you only talk to someone about one subject and then leave, the person will feel as if they did something to offend you or something like that. You do not want to leave anyone feeling that way.

The best way to avoid that is to make sure that you keep the conversation going to the point where it would be safe to exit without offending the person you are talking too. This section will help you more understand how to keep a conversation going and keep it going well.

Tip Three- Self Disclosure

To understand this advice, there is going to have to be some in-depth explanation of what self-disclosure is. To save you from having to look it up, this tip will include all the information you need to know about it. Of course, that will make this trip a lot longer, but it is better to have a long tip that you understand than a short briefing on something that leaves you confused.

Self-disclosure is where you add to a conversation by giving the other person information about yourself. This is a hard thing to do, as most people worry about boring others with talk of themselves, or they are afraid to seem conceited.

There are two dimensions to self-disclosure. They are breadth and depth. These are both essential to holding a good conversation, and connecting with the person you are talking to. You want to be able to connect with the people around you or else you will not be able to hold a genuine and meaningful conversation. You have to have both to enable the act of self-disclosure indeed.

The breadth of self-disclosure refers to the range of topics you discuss when opening up about yourself. No, you don't have to disclose your deepest darkest secrets, but giving someone a little bit of information about several different subjects about yourself allows them to feel a little closer to you, thus enabling them to open up about themselves. This helps extend the conversation and lets the person feel values as if you are interested in talking with them. Try starting with the easiest topics, such as interests, and move on to schooling, and views on the world. The more subjects you cover, the longer the conversation will be, and the more you will be able to connect with the person you are talking too.

Depth is slightly harder to reach. Now if you are just chatting up with someone you don't plan to develop a deep friendship with, you can almost skip depth, but a deep conversation is necessary for those you wish to establish a real friendship with. However, even in a simple conversation, you need to have some depth to what you are saying. Tell them about the time you broke your arm in third grade, or something of the like. Give them a memory to make them feel as if you care about the conversation you are having, and are not just chatting to pass the time.

The act of self-disclosure is a type of social penetration. This is a theory that you can only establish any relationship, whether it be romantic or platonic, by communication. But not just any type of communication, systematically fluid conversation. This means that over time, you let the person in more and more, and you change the direction of your conversation regularly to establish a connection with the individual you are communicating with.

You also have to allow time for the person to reciprocate in the conversation. Don't spend the entire time talking about yourself. If you are worried about droning on too long about what you like and such, try employing the one detail method. This means that you share a detail about yourself, and let the other person share a detail about themselves. Continue this on until you find a happy medium between not sharing enough and talking too much.

As you can see self-disclosure is critical, as you need to allow, a person to feel as if you are invested in the conversation. If you do not seem like you care to talk to them, they will close off, and not want to talk much more than the basic hello followed by an icebreaker subject. So how do you efficiently employ this technique?

1. **Start Small:** On top of them feeling like you are interested, they also have to be interested in what you have to say. Rather than unloading a whole pile of information on someone that doesn't

care, start with a small bit of information to see if they take the bait. If you use the icebreaker about music, try telling them your favorite song, and explaining a final reason for why you love it. If they just give you a one-word reply, it is best to duck out of the conversation then. They don't care. However, if they seem interested, and ask you, more then you can start talking about more of your interests and such.

2. **Decide on The Type of Conversation:** You should always try to approach every conversation as if you seek to make a new friend. However, if you are at a convention with people from around the globe, chances are you are not going to establish a life-long friendship. You should still show interest in the individual, but that would impact the type of information that you are going to divulge. You don't want someone you are never going to see again knowing a deep secret about you. Instead, tell them about childhood memories that you don't feel would impact how they think of you. Your favorite thing to do as a child or stuff like that. Those are safe subjects for people who you are just talking to at that moment.

3. **Skim the Surface:** You want people to be interested in you for a long time. This means that you cannot divulge everything about you in one conversation. You have to be conservative with your information. The best way to do this is to take a little bit of information from many different subjects to talk about. As you get to know a person more and more, you can add more details to that. This helps you also ensure that you are not talking about yourself too much.

4. **Allow Reciprocation:** The best part of self-disclosure is that it allows the other person a gateway to say themselves as well. You don't want to hog the stage and only talk about yourself. You want to keep the flow of information even. Give the other person some time to tell you about themselves as well. The conversation will come alight as you are swapping stories and some fun little tidbits of information about yourself.

5. **Be Loose:** Telling someone about yourself should be done with ease. You don't want to sound like someone who is selling something, though in reality that is what you are doing in a way. You are trying to convince the person to like you with the truth. However, it should not sound like you are a documentary. You should be light and airy when talking about yourself. Make the person interested. Intrigue them, and draw them in, get them want to know more about you.

6. **Timing:** Just like when you deliver the punchline to a joke, it is all about the timing. You have to time the information that you provide. This is a little tricky if you don't know what goes into timing a deliverance. There has to be a level of interest from the other person. To ensure that you have their interest, you have to make them ask a few questions. You can't just offer up all the information. However, you can't make them pry every bit of info from you either. There has to be a give and take kind of flow going on there.

7. **Caution:** There are some things that you do not tell a person you just met. It may seem like you have known the person

forever, but you still have to use caution when divulging certain things. For example, if you were a former addict, it is best not to mention it unless necessary. You do not want anything to skew how they think of you until they get to know you. If you are confident in yourself, however, then try divulging that info. What you are cautious with depends on you.

There you have it. Self-disclosure at its finest. This is one of the most important things to holding a good conversation. Now, remember, your entire conversation does not have to consist of self-disclosure alone, but throwing in a few facts here and there go a long way. Make sure you utilize this to the fullest advantage possible.

Tip Four- Engage the Other Person Fully

Part of the problem these days is that conversation becomes one sided. Even though both parties are speaking, they are not really in the conversation. They are not properly engaging the other person. This is a big issue when communication relies entirely on both parties being actively involved in the discussion to allow it to succeed. If you are not actively engaging the other person, and not participating yourself, then you will fall flat in the conversation.

First off, how you can be engaged in the conversation better, without taking it over.

1. **Actively Listen:** No one wants to feel like they are talking to a brick wall. They want to feel like the person they are talking to is genuinely interested in what they have to say. This means that you have to listen to understand. Today's generation teaches

you to hear the reply, and that is where the problem lies. By only looking to respond, you are not processing what the other person is saying because your mind is on yourself. This is a selfish, bad habit that this day and age has taken to sticking too.

2. **Reply with Interest:** Even if you are not quite interested in what the other person is talking about, you should always respond with interest. It is polite, and even though you may not be interested in it now, you might gain some interesting knowledge by listening to what they have to say. You can't just expect everyone to have the same interests as you, and there are probably things that you like that others do not like but they still act like they are at least interested in it, because it is the polite thing to do.

3. **Ask Questions:** Asking questions to get more information about what they are talking about shows the other person that you were listening, and that you want to know more. It allows the person to be relieved because then they do not feel like they are boring you with their information. The only way that they know that you are interested is if you are asking questions. Then they know that it is okay to continue talking about the subject they are on.

4. **Be THERE:** I know it can be hard if someone is droning on and on about something that you have no interest in, but it is still good etiquette to be there mentally. This means that when someone is talking, don't let your mind go on vacation, and tune the person out because if you are that disinterested in them, it is

more polite to change the subject rather than just leave the conversation mentally.

That is how you can be engaged in a conversation. Following these tips will allow you to breathe easier knowing that you are pleasantly talking to a person, and you won't offend them because you seem disinterested. You just have to practice these things, because sometimes it can be a little tricky.

How to Engage Them

1. **Be Interesting:** This does not mean you have to make up stories. It has nothing to do with the information you are giving at all. You just have to deliver it in an interesting way. You could tell someone you climbed Mount Everest on the back of Dwayne Johnson, and if you inform the story in a monotone voice, it will sound dull. It is not what you are saying; it is how you are saying. Tell them your stories as if you were telling them for the first time. Be engaged yourself, and show the person that you want them to talk to you. You want their attention. Only then will you get the attention you so desire.

2. **Leave Openings:** Even without using self-disclosure, you still have to leave openings for the other person to talk, no matter the subject. No one wants to stand there and listen to someone take control of the conversation. You might as well be talking to yourself for that matter. Or to the plant in the corner. You have to let the other person talk as well. A good conversation allows both parties to talk equally and without any hitches. It is

not people talking about everything while the other person stands there and nods.

3. **Allow Questions:** If a person asks a question, don't dodge it. This should not have to be said, but a lot of people avoid questions for fear of sounding conceited, but in truth, you just seem rude. If someone is asking a question, you are not going to sound pretentious by answering it. If you dodge a question, the person will feel as if they offended you, and they will be less likely to stay engaged in the conversation.

That is how you engage someone in conversation. It is a lot easier than staying involved in a discussion as long as they are interested in what is being said. All you have to do is be open and friendly, and let the rest fall into place.

How These Tips Help

These tips are designed to help you keep a conversation going without being nervous. These tips also contribute to improving your communication skills. By using these tips, you will feel more comfortable having a longer conversation with someone that you just met than you would be if you were just trying to find things to talk about.

These tips will give you the boost you need to feel confident in your abilities to talk to people and enjoy the conversation without having to worry every second that you are saying something wrong.

Chapter 4: Getting Through a Conversation

These tips are for what you should do during and after a conversation with someone. They are tips on how to properly act when communicating, as there is often some confusion about what to do especially now that it is no longer a curriculum at school or home. Do not fret. This book will clarify that right up.

Tip Five- Etiquette During a Conversation

It is of utmost importance that you have the proper etiquette when talking to someone. The key to holding a good conversation is not to offend them and to show them that you are a real person to talk to. You want to keep their attention and let them know that they have yours. Otherwise, you will not get very far in the communication realm, as people will not want to talk to you, thinking you are rude.

So it is best to study up on proper etiquette before you put yourself out there. While most of these are common sense, they are in here just in case nerves cause a problem with combining common sense with communication. That is a real issue a lot of people have. They cannot rely on their common sense because they are too nervous to remember to use it.

So here are the etiquette rules to help you out. Remember, a slip up is okay as long as you don't do it continually, but it is best to try to be as clean cut as possible to avoid any issues.

1. **Handshake:** This is the first thing you should do, as you say hello. Unless the person is germaphobic, or you are, not

offering a handshake is considered rude. If you do have a phobia of germs, it is best to explain that as you are saying hello, so there are no misunderstandings. Make sure that they know that you are still pleased to meet them; you just would rather not shake their hand. Most people can be pretty understanding.

The perfect handshake is firm but pliant. You can't grip too tight, because you are not trying to intimidate someone, and a grip too loose makes people feel that you are not that thrilled to meet them, and are only doing so out of necessity. This is not a great first impression, as people want to feel like they are worth getting to know. So it is best to make sure you give a real, genuine handshake.

2. **Eye Contact:** This one is important to maintain from the beginning to end. It is always disconcerting to talk to someone who is looking off into the distance or anywhere else but who is talking to them. (autistic people are not counted in this, nor are the ocularly impaired) Eye contact shows that you are paying attention to them. To show you why eye contact is so important, let us have a mini history lesson.

Back in the time of extreme social hierarchy, where people who made less money than you were deemed undesirable, eye contact was a way of establishing that social ladder. Anyone who was considered below you had to make eye contact with you, while you were not to make eye contact with them. To make eye contact with a person deemed lowly, put you on their level, and could cause you to lose your social position if caught.

Kings never looked anyone but other kings in the eye, no one ever made eye contact with serfs other than other serfs. Men did not make eye contact with women, as even women were deemed below them. They only time someone made eye contact with a lady that was not another woman, was a servant, or a peasant to a duchess or queen. Eye contact was the primary factor of social hierarchy

By not looking someone in the eye during a conversation, you are essentially saying that they are beneath you and that what they have to say is n't matter. That may not be what you are trying to do, but that is the message you are portraying when you refuse to look someone in the eye.

3. Body Language: This will be more brushed on in a later chapter, but it also falls under etiquette. You have to have an open body language in a conversation. Otherwise, you risk making a person feel as if you are unapproachable, and not open to discussion. You can also make them feel as if what they are saying has no value. You can do so much damage with a few simple gestures, and this is a problem. You have to be careful with your stance and make sure that you are not closing yourself off.

4. No Phone: This should go without saying, but if your phone goes off, DON'T ANSWER IT! Society today is so caught up in the conversations that they have going on on the other side of the screen, that they forget the importance of conversation

with the person on the other aspect of the table. You are in a real time conversation with a real person. (Not that the person texting you isn't real, but they are not there.) The best thing to do is to put your phone on silent if you know you are going to talk to people. That way you do not feel tempted to pull it out and text rather than speaking with those around you.

Cell phones are a wonderfully destructive device. They can help you connect with people from around the world, but unfortunately, that causes you to disconnect from the people that are right next to you. A lot of people use their phone as a crutch to not have to talk to people when they feel uncomfortable. This does not help you in any way. They only way to become comfortable with a situation is to put yourself out there and talk to people. Find someone to talk to and eventually you will take your mind off of the fact that you are anxious about being around people.

5. Don't Interrupt: When someone is talking to you, it is best to stay quiet until you are sure they have finished what they are saying. You have to be very careful when talking to someone that you are listening to them, and not listening to respond. This is one of the biggest problems in today's conversations. No one looks to people for more than knowing when to jump in and reply. This leads to more people interrupting, which often angers the other person, and makes them not want to talk to you any longer.

Listen to the person, and remember that you would not want to be interrupted. No one likes to be talked over, and no one likes talking to someone who constantly does it. Be patient. Your time to talk will come.

6. Personal Space: This is a big one. A lot of people get really close to people when they are talking. This is uncomfortable for the other person. You have to make sure that you keep a safe distance between you and the other person. Arm's length apart is a good chatting distance unless you are in a loud place, and then from forearm length apart is usually as close as you should be. If it is too loud to hear, then you should hold the conversation until you are in a quieter environment.

Claustrophobia is a big problem for a vast majority of a population. Invading someone's personal space can make them very uncomfortable. You have to respect that people need personal space when talking to you. Even if they don't have claustrophobia, it is still gross when someone is so close to you that you can feel their spit as they are talking. Keep the distance.

7. Get Close: This may seem to contradict the last statement, but you have to be close enough that it does not look like you are trying to escape the conversation. However, it is not that contradictory. You just have to find a happy medium. You want to be close enough that the other person is not sniffing themselves trying to figure out if it is them, but you have to be far enough away that you are not crowding their personal space.

A good indicator is your arms. Of course, you do not physically stretch them out to see if you are standing close enough, but rather you visualize where you are at. You should never be so close that you have to bend your arm at more than a ninety-degree angle to touch them, but you should not be so far away that when your arms are fully outstretched your palms can't rest on their shoulders. Try to stay in that golden circle of space, and you should be good.

Those are the tips for etiquette during a conversation. Follow these, and you should have no problem with people not wanting to talk to you. You will make the other person feel respected, and that is what you are striving for.

Tip Six- Etiquette When Leaving a Conversation

1. Timing: As stated before, timing is everything when talking to people. You have to be good at your timing and actually, know when to say something when not to say something. In this case, timing has to do with when to exit a conversation. No matter how good a conversation has been, you begin to wear out your welcome. If a person starts to look around or shift about, they are probably ready to go or do something else. This is your cue to end the conversation if they do not. Finish what you were saying, and then use an exit phrase such as "Oh I can't believe how much of your time I have taken! It was so great talking to you I just got swept up at the moment!" Make them feel good while ending the conversation.

2. Ending Phrase: As mentioned in the above bullet, you have to use a good ending phrase to make the person feel as if the conversation end is not their fault, even if it is. Be polite, and make them feel like you were so enthralled by talking to them that you regret having to end the conversation, but you do not want to take up any more of their time. This will make them feel valued, and that will get them want to talk to you again.

3. Ask for Contact Info: If you have the chance of seeing someone again, or just would like to stay in touch, ask if they would like to exchange contact information. If they say yes, go ahead and give them your number and ask for theirs, giving a test call to make sure you input the number right and allowing them to be sure of the same, as the will have your number on the call. If they do not wish to exchange information, do not push. It doesn't mean you did anything wrong; they just may not think that they will see you again. That is okay.

Always ask if they want to exchange information. It is a lot more comfortable for them, as it gives them a little more room to say no without feeling bad. Asking them for their contact information directly does not allow for them to say no without feeling bad because you assumed that they wanted to. Remember, the right conversation does not mean they have to become your best friend. A lot of people get so attached to someone they had a single enthralling conversation with, that they are upset when the person does not want to keep in touch. This is only human nature, as we are designed to communicate for survival. Breaking yourself of this habit will be difficult, but if you do it, you will be less affected by the rejection you feel when someone does not wish to stay in touch.

4. Follow Up: This only refers to people who exchanged info. If they give you their contact information, then text or call them the next day to see how they are doing and let them know that you were serious about wanting to stay in touch. Make the person feel important, but only text once, and let them respond. They might be busy when you try to reach them and will get back to you later.

These are the etiquette rules for ending a conversation. If you use them, you can be confident that you are not leaving someone with awkwardness in the air.

How These Tips Help

These tips give you the boost up in a conversation to show a person that you are respectful, and that you have proper manners. This will make them enjoy talking to you a lot better than if you did not know these rules.

Etiquette is slowly slipping away, by trying to bring it back, you will also start a ripple effect, as the person you are talking to will pick up on these social cues, and start using them in their conversations with others. By doing this little simple thing, you can help bring proper communication etiquette back into a trend.

Chapter 5: Additional Tips

These tips are just extra tips that you should know and insert throughout different conversations. They do not necessarily have to apply to every conversation, as they are not about the conversation itself, but how to psych yourself up to talk to people, and how to handle rejection without letting it ruin you.

Tip Seven- Get Out of Your Head

You have to get out of your own head to ever hold a good conversation with someone because you have to be able to approach someone to talk to them. If you are stuck in your head, and the "Oh I can't" thoughts, then you will be stuck at only talking to people you have to.

By getting out of your head, you will feel confident enough to approach a person that you have never met before, and that has no correlation to any of your friends. This is the best feeling, knowing that you can make friends anywhere, and not have to worry about going somewhere and not knowing anyone there.

Imagine you are going to a party. Your friend says that they will meet you there. You are glad, because you don't know anyone else who will be attending, or they are just minor acquaintances from work or school. You get there, and your friend texts you were saying that they can't come because something came up. You don't panic because you decide just to go find someone to talk to. You walk up to a guy or girl you have never seen before and strike up a conversation. Before the night is up, you have met seven new people that you really get along with.

That is what can happen once you stop the thoughts that you aren't good enough to talk to someone, or that you are too boring for anyone to want to talk to. Confidence is key. Boost yourself up, and as they say, fake it till you make it. You have to boost yourself up because there is not going to be anyone in the world who is able to make you feel better about yourself than you can. Go in with the mindset that you are worth talking to, and that you are funny and witty. By believing in yourself, people will be more open to you, as they can see that you are confident in yourself.

Tip Eight- Boost Your Self Esteem

This one goes hand in hand with getting out of your head. You have to believe in yourself to get out of your head. If you have low self-esteem, you will be more prone to rejection, because just like lions, people can pick out the ugly ones. No one wants to have to carry the entire conversation, so they generally steer away from the shy people, and gravitate to someone who they know will actively engage in conversation.

The way to boost your self-esteem can also involve a mirror. Stand in front of it for ten minutes a day only saying positive things about yourself. You are smart; you are strong, you are caring, you are kind. Do not mention any of your negative attributes. For every negative thing you say, add another minute to the time you spend looking in the mirror. It is your responsibility to build yourself up, no one else's. You can do it. As the days go on, you will find you are having to add less time onto your ten minutes, until finally, you spend just the ten minutes saying entirely positive things about yourself. Eventually, you will begin to believe them. You are essentially retraining your brain to say nice things to you, rather than mean things.

This society is so bleak, and some so many mean people say hateful things while hiding behind a computer screen, and this has cause self-esteem rates to go way down. Build yourself back up to stay above the hatred

Tip Nine- Handle Rejection with Pride

If you have low self-esteem, this will be hard, so you have to build yourself up to be able to do this. Otherwise, it will get to you, and make you not want to talk to people any longer. If you are rejected before you build yourself up, just take some time to recuperate.

Not everyone will want to talk to you, especially nowadays. In today's age, people judge others before they even open their mouths, and decide on if a person is "worthy" of speaking to them. You have to break away from this thinking. You also cannot think that someone is above your level, they may seem like they are, and turn out to be the nicest person ever. However, when you approach someone, they may reject you, and this is okay. You may not want to talk to anyone that approaches you either.

If you are rejected, shake it off. Remind yourself that it is not you, it is who they are. They decided that they did not want to get to know you, and that is their loss, not yours. Get back up on that metaphorical horse and try again with someone else. You will find someone who is actually worth talking to.

Tip Ten- Don't Latch On

In a setting with a lot of people, it is so easy to try to find people that you enjoy talking to and staying with them a majority of the time. This is not a superb idea. You have to work for the crowd so to speak. How boring would it be if you were at a concert, and the singer only interacted with one fan? It is the same concept with talking to people. Go around to different people, and try to make more than one new friend. Eventually, you can come back to that one person, but let them have some time to talk to others, and give yourself time to talk to others as well.

How These Tips Help

These tips are for your own personal use to adapt to specific conversations and situation, and to psych yourself up before you go to a social event where you may not know someone that is there.

Following these tips will give you an edge on your conversations. Using these will help give you a self-esteem boost, and you will learn how to help yourself. These tips will make you a better conversationalist and a better you.

Chapter 6: After the Tips

If you have tried all of these tips, and find that you still cannot connect with people, you should try to see about getting some help with a psychiatrist. There could be some real deep-seated issues there. Talking to people is hard, but if you have tried to break out of your shell, and find yourself having panic attacks every time, you need to know what is going wrong.

There is nothing wrong with getting help either. Just as you would need to see a doctor for a physical illness, you should see a psychiatrist if your social anxiety is so bad that it is causing you to break down at the thought of talking to someone you do not know. There are a lot of resources that are at your disposal. If you are not sure a psychiatrist in your area, try talking to your average doctor, and he can help refer you to someone. The best thing about that is he is more likely to know a specialist to ensure that you are getting the best level of help that you can get.

How to know if it is more than just being shy

- You have panic attacks regularly in social situations: This can be the sign of a serious problem. You should get it checked out, and maybe the doctor can help you figure out how to work through it in a way that is best suited to you.

- You avoid stores during busy hours: If you would rather go without a necessity for a period of time because you do not want to visit a store during working hours as there will be too many people there, and could cause you to have a meltdown, you should see a doctor. This is serious. You cannot deny your needs. A physician can help you figure out the root of the problem, and set you on your way to healing.

- If you feel physically ill in social situations where there are only a handful of people: If being in small groups makes you feel physically ill, you should definitely look into it. Doing so allows you to truly live your life to the fullest, once you figure out what is wrong.

Don't let anxiety control your life any longer. Get the help you deserve and do not feel bad for doing so. You deserve to live a happy life unrestrained by anxiety. Regain control of your life.

PART VII

CHAPTER 1

WHAT ARE THESE SECRET KEYS TO A

RELATIONSHIP BREAKTHROUGH?

Have you ever wondered why so many people fail in their relationship with men, whether as friends or more than that? Wondered why so many couples break up, even though it seemed like they would be together forever? Do you have a hard time connecting with men enough to take your relationship to the highest level possible? Many people do, and that is because they do not know about these secret keys for a breakthrough.

It is essential to know what men want and need, otherwise, you will not be able to know him as well as you wish you could, and the distance will make it hard to connect. A connection is important when in a relationship, as it is what determines the amount of passion you have years down the road. A weak connection makes for weak passion and limited intimacy once the honeymoon phase is over.

If you do not have passion and intimacy in a marriage, this can be a major problem, as they are what keep the love alive, and the marriage interesting. Without any interest in your marriage, it can cause many problems, including divorce, and infidelity.

So to avoid these issues you must learn about the secret keys, for without them you will be destined to have an average relationship, rather than a superb relationship. Which an average one can last forever, but a superb relationship will most definitely last forever.

Only about twenty percent of people know about these keys to a man's heart. They are the couples that you see that are eighty years old and still acting like young lovers. They are the couples that everyone aspires to be. These people are the happiest couples alive because they learned the secret keys to marriage, and to unlock their man's heart.

Why it is Pertinent to Know these Keys

These keys are the basis of obtaining a strong and intimate relationship. Almost everyone's goal in life is to get married, and have that marriage last forever. They want to be the couple that everyone looks up to, and that everyone comes to for advice.

That is where these keys come in. They are designed to help you achieve that level of a relationship in your life. These are from a man's perspective, to help you understand more what they really want. Not what women say they want.

A man's heart is unique. It is unlike a woman's heart in many ways, and should be treated as such. You should want to know exactly how to open his heart to show you exactly how he wants to be loved.

Men are also stubborn at times. You may have already won his heart, but he has put up walls to try to prevent himself from falling. You have to break through these walls as well, which if you use these keys, should be easier than just whacking away at it with charm. Read on to find these keys.

Chapter 2:

Secret Key #1

Desire

Men do not say this aloud, which is why this key is such a big secret, but men love romance. They want their partners to put in a little romantic effort as well. This key is important, as without it, a man cannot be sure if you are really down for him or not. If he doesn't feel like you desire him, he will not completely open up to you. Very few couples realize how important this is, and that is why often times, you see relationships fizzle out so fast. Follow this key to strengthen your bond with the male species.

Romance

Describe your most romantic fantasy. Is it elaborate? Or simple? Either way, you most likely still have one. So does he. Men are romantic creatures by nature, but they also like to be romanced. Take him out to dinner, and pick up the check. Take him out to the movies, and pay for him. Return the favor he probably often shows you quite frequently.

It doesn't even have to be that expensive either. When he has a long day at work, surprise him with his favorite dinner served by candlelight. In his day off, pack a picnic lunch, and drive to his favorite spot and enjoy a picnic. It doesn't have to always be fancy, you just need to put in as much effort into showing him you want him, as he does for you.

It is about feeling wanted, and loved. If you aren't putting in an effort to show him how much you care, how is he going to know that you are going to be there in the long run? He will feel like you are only there for what he can do for you, not what you can do together, and he will begin to feel used. Value a man. Don't expect to get treated like royalty if you are only going to treat him like a peasant.

To understand more about being romantic for a guy, this scenario will help you to understand more, that it isn't always about the big things, sometimes even the smallest gesture means the world to a guy.

Scenario

James looked over at his girlfriend, and wondered if she truly loved him. She said it all the time, but how did he know for sure? Was she just fronting to get his money or was she truly his ride or die chick? How could he be sure that she really loved him?

"Babe?" He called over to MaryBeth

"Yes, baby?" She replied

"Answer three questions for me. What is my favorite color? What was my favorite memory as a child? What is my favorite food?" James needed to know if she loved him as much as he loved her. He knew that her favorite color was purple, because it reminded her of the twilight hours when everything is quiet and still. He knew that her favorite childhood memory was when her dad took some free bikes and pieced them together to make her very first bike because they were too poor to buy a new one. He knew that her favorite food was Italian, and that it only became so when she met him, because he was Italian, and showed her how real cuisine was created, rather than restaurants that order frozen food and heat it up in a microwave. He wanted to see if she knew the answers to those questions.

"You don't have a favorite color, per say. You are color blind. You say that your favorite color would be emerald green because that is the color I told you my eyes were. Your favorite childhood memory was when you and your brother climbed the big oak tree in your backyard together, and talked about life and what your plans were for your futures. You said that was the first time you two had really ever bonded, and that was when you realized you wanted to be a real estate investor. You were nine. Your favorite food is Chinese, because it reminds you of when your mother used to take you to a Chinese restaurant every Friday for mother-son bonding time. The last time you did that with her was two days before she died. You used to dislike Chinese food, but went because she loved it, but after she died, the memories made you love it." She answered. "Now tell me. What is this about?"

"I was wondering if you loved me. No girl has ever paid enough attention to me, and focused mainly on my wallet. You answered every question perfectly. The first one to ever do so. I love you so much."

"How could you doubt I love you, James? I may not have a lot of money, but I try to show you every day that I love you. You should think about that, rather than focusing on little questions that anyone who pays attention to you could answer." MaryBeth replied, slightly offended that he felt she didn't love him.

As she walked out of the room, James sat and thought about what she said. He thought back over the course of their relationship, and thought about all the things she did for him regularly.

She cooks me dinner on a regular basis. When I have had a hard day, she rubs my back. Even though she is on her feet for over eight hours a day, and mine is just stress of a tenant not wanting to pay rent. She shows up on my longer days with my favorite meal, and we eat it together before we have to go back to work. For no reason at all, she told me to get in the car, and we drove to our favorite spot with some fast food, and ate while watching the trains pull into the station.

She always tells me she loves me before she goes to bed, even if she is angry with me. She never fails to ask me how my day was, and truly listen to the answer. Even though sometimes I tune her out when she talks about hers. I don't know what her favorite song is, or when her first heartbreak happened, but she sure as hell know mine. What have I done for her? I know the answer to three questions that anyone with half a brain could answer, and I buy her stuff. I take her out to fancy dinners, and spend money on her but that is about it, and yet she never questions my love for her. I want to marry this woman. She is my everything. She has a piece of me that no one else ever will. She truly has my heart.

James walked back into the bedroom, where he found MaryBeth crying. He sat beside her, and began to rub her back.

"I'm sorry. I am so sorry I ever doubted your love for me. I know I could say that every other girlfriend has only wanted my money, and it broke me, but in truth; I am just an ass. I love you, MaryBeth. I want to marry you someday. Not today, we still have a lot of things to work through, but if you forgive me, I promise that one day you will have an engagement ring on your finger." James said, pulling out a little ring and sliding it on her ring finger. "Do you accept my promise?"

"Yes. I forgive you as well." MaryBeth said, beaming with happiness while her eyes were still brimming with tears.

Discussion

James didn't realize until it was brought to his attention, all the little things that MaryBeth does for him to show her love. Sometimes you do have to give him a little wake up call to show him that you do play the romance card on a regular basis. Maybe do a big gesture here and there to really show him you care. But sometimes it just takes you telling him to think that gets his brain in gear. Be romantic, and even if he doesn't realize it at first, he will start to see all the little things you do for him, even when he doesn't notice you doing them.

Desire

You have to ignite a white-hot passion in him that makes him want to take you right here and right now almost any where you go. This desire is what fuels the passion in your relationship. If there is no passion, things get stale, and that is when people drift apart the most. If the bedroom isn't rocking, you better get packing, because you need a good sex life, and desire filled relationship to last for a long time.

How do you ignite this desire in him? It is simple. You have to desire him as well. Men are easily enticed, if you are willing to tap into your animalistic nature. You have to want to make him desire you, so that means you will have to be pro-active in your sexuality, and prove your prowess in the bedroom, along with outside the bedroom.

How is this done exactly? Ditch the missionary position. This is the bane of all sexual existence. There are so many more positions out there, where you don't have to lie there like a lifeless doll and take what he is giving you. (Ditch standard doggy style for gay couples. This is the missionary in the gay world.) Look up new positions and try them for yourselves. Try different styles. There are some that can spice up the bedroom if you are both willing to try it.

- BDSM: This is a type of sexual style that requires one partner to be dominant, and one partner to be submissive. Start out slow. Don't go "Fifty Shades of Grey" level the first day. Ease into it. Find out the limitations your bodies can handle, how tight you like the collars and ties, what you absolutely do not like, and so on and so forth. Knowing what you like is important, as if you don't like it, the experience will not be fun. Both of you have to be vocal if you want to know what each other likes and don't like. Also, come up with a safe word to use, so in the heat of the moment, you don't hurt yourselves.

- Roleplay: This is one for when you want to experience what it is like to have sex with someone different, yet still wanting that sex to be with your partner. You get little costumes, and you dress up as someone else. While dressed up as another person, you literally become that person. You are not yourself, you are a whole other person. This could mean you have your guy become the cable guy, or you become his secretary. There are many other people you can take on the role of, such as famous people, or make up your own personas. If you do not feel comfortable with role play, but are still intrigued by it, try it on a small scale. Have him be a fake person you make up, and vice versa. This will get you more comfortable with the idea, so you can more enjoy it.

- Making a Home Video: This can be a very good bonding experience in the bedroom, as you can watch back the video you make, and see how much you were enjoying the sex. Once you both realize how good things are in the bedroom, you will never want to leave. Relax and enjoy it, though. Don't try to put on a show just because you are being filmed. You aren't a porn star, and neither is he. Just enjoy it. You can also see what positions work for you, and what doesn't when you play the video back. These videos should never be put on the internet, or used for any other reason than your viewing pleasure. If handled correctly, they can make for great material to get you in the mood as well.

- Watch Porn Together: This can give you an idea on positions to try, and also get you in the mood to do the deed. Find a video that you both like, and settle in. You can also try a bit of self stimulation while watching the video, but be careful not to distract yourself, or your partner from the video itself. The whole point is to learn new positions and bond. Remember though, porn is an act. Do not expect to have super explosive orgasms the first time you try a position. You most likely will have to practice a few times for it to even feel good.

There are many ways to spark up some interest in the bedroom, but how do you make him want to do these things? How do you spark the carnal desire in him? How do you show him you want him so bad it makes your stomach do flips? There are a few ways that are fool proof.

- Send Him Little Notes: You can leave sticky notes all over the house for him, in his car, in his lunchbox if he has one. You can also text him all the things you would like to do to him. Tell him that you aren't wearing any underwear or something like that. Give him something to want later that night.

- Tease Him: Kiss him seductively in the hall way and then keep moving along. Rub your rear against his junk, and then walk away. Play footsie with him when you eat dinner. Make him desire you, turn him on, but then leave him hanging. At the end of the night he will want you so bad, he will do anything to have you.

- Be Playful: Sometimes the biggest turn on is when you act like a kid. Being free-spirited can be the biggest turn on for guys, because they like knowing you are happy and having fun. Tickle him, and then make him chase you to the bedroom and tackle you on the bed. Play wrestle a little bit, and watch the playing turn into sex real fast. Sometimes the best foreplay, is to simply play.

You have to create a white-hot desire in the pit of his stomach, one that makes him crave you when you are away, and not want to leave your side when you are near. You have to make him think about you constantly, to the point where he doesn't even want you to go to the restroom because that means being away from you for too long.

This desire will unlock the part of his heart that makes him want to commit. He won't want to leave, because he is too devoted to you, and he loves you way too much to walk away from everything you have together. You have to keep this desire alive, and strong, to keep the relationship strong and healthy.

Here is a scenario that should help you get a mental picture of what that desire looks like. Caution. This one is mildly graphic, but if you are an adult reading this, as the disclaimer warns, you have probably read much worse.

Scenario

He wanted her. He wanted her more than he has ever wanted anyone. The way she teased him drove him insane. It was like she took pleasure in keeping him aroused to the point of pain. She would pay for it, when she finally let him have her. These thoughts swirled around Mason's brain, and left him winded. He thought back to when they first met.

Lacy wasn't like a lot of girls. That is what attracted Mason to her. He was tired of girls throwing themselves at him. He was tired of girls who had nothing more to offer than a loose vagina, and some amateur head. These women bored Mason, so he never kept them around much longer than a night. Lacy, however, showed very little interest in Mason when they first met. She looked him up and down, offered her hand in a professional manner, and said it was nice to meet him. Like she was at a job interview. She didn't blush, or swoon, or make any indication that she found Mason attractive. He had to have her. She was exactly what he wanted. A challenging woman.

He became more and more infatuated with her as the night drew on, and he listened to her talk, and engaged in conversation with her. She was Harvard educated, and it showed. She wasn't haughty or anything, really she was very humble, but when she spoke her words were eloquent and well thought out. She didn't use 'like' in between every word, as most girls tend to do. Instead, every word out of her mouth was carefully planted like she was speaking a puzzle.

She turned him on. Plain, and simple. He had to have a date with her.

"Excuse me, Lacy? I am enamored by your eloquence, and would love to talk to you more, one-on-one. Would you care to have a cup of coffee with me after this party is over?" Mason asked

"Why don't we leave right now? I feel I am boring everyone else." Lacy said

"I highly doubt you are boring anyone, but if you wish, I would love to go at once."

They left the club, and walked down the street to a little coffee shop that was open twenty four hours a day. This was one of Mason's spots to think, and he wanted Lacy to experience it as well. When they walked in, he could tell that she was star-struck with the place. It wasn't well known, but it was cozy. He offered to buy her coffee, but she refused, stating that she was glad to have an excuse to leave the club.

"I hope you don't think that I am like other girls, Mason." Lacy said as soon as the found a cozy nook to sit down.

"I beg you are pardon?" Mason nearly choked on his latte

"I don't put out on the first date. You have to win my heart. You can't just bring me to a quaint little coffee shop, and expect me to sleep with you tonight." Lacy was blunt with what she spoke, there was no beating around the bush.

"Of course I don't think you are like other girls. In fact, I have never brought a woman here before."

As if on cue, the shop owner came out then to greet Mason.

"Mason, my old friend. Are you enjoying your evening? Oh! You have a lady with you! Forgive me for interrupting, I have never seen this before. Enjoy yourselves." The shop owner ducked back into his office with a bright red face.

"Well I guess I don't need to ask you to prove that you have never brought a woman here."

They sat and talked the night away. In the wee hours of the morning, Mason drove Lacy home, as her friends had already left the club.

"Lacy, can I see you again?" Mason asked, as she stepped out of the car.

"I would like that very much."

Three months later, Lacy practically lived with him. They often slept in the same bed. And he still had not been able to make love to her. That is what he wanted. He didn't want to just have sex with her, he wanted to make love to her.

"What is on your mind, Mace?" Lacy asked, sitting on his lap.

"I want you, Lacy. More than I have ever wanted anyone. I love you. I truly love you. I want to make passionate love to you, in a way no man ever has. I want to give you the world, if you will let me. You are the one I want. Forever."

"Mason, that is what I have been wanting to hear since we met. Tonight you will finally get what you want. Me."

That night was the most mind blowing night of Mason's life. Lacy felt perfect for him. They didn't leave the bedroom for hours. Everything was perfect.

Flash forward two years later, and Lacy still teased him. He still wanted her as much as he did from day one. He couldn't imagine life with any other woman, as she was the only one who lit such a desire in him.

Discussion

Lacy made Mason desire her, by not always being readily available. She let him know she was into him, but she did not give up everything from the beginning, and even after she gave it all up, she still kept that playfulness up in the relationship, making him want her bad enough to always desire her.

This is what you have to do in a relationship. You have to keep your partner interested in you. Don't think that just because you have been together for a long time, that means you have to act like an old couple. Be playful. Show each other how much you care.

Chapter 3:

Secret Key #2

Make Him Feel Safe

Men will never admit that they need to feel safe in a relationship. This key is a secret, because society makes men feel that they have to be macho all the time. This is the furthest from the truth, and you should not believe this, as everyone needs to feel safe. Not just physically, but emotionally.

Couples that know this often have less fights, and less time spent angry at each other. Fights and arguments do not stem from someone doing something that you don't agree with, they stem from being afraid that they are going to leave you. You get angry because you don't feel safe, and you are scared you are going to be left alone, so you throw up a wall. Men do the same thing as everyone else. Only they will never admit that is why they have a wall up.

You have to make him want to take all of his walls down and be open with you. Make him feel like you want to know everything about him. Not just where he grew up, what his favorite color is, and what music does he like. Ask him if he ever sucked his thumb, did he have a teddy bear or a blankie? What was his favorite television show growing up? Has he ever been in trouble? What are his aspirations, and fears? Ask him about his nightmares. Do not be satisfied with one word answers. Give him information about you every time he divulges something about himself.

Emotional Safety

You have to be his safety net as he is free-falling into love with you, just as he has to be yours. You have to catch each other, and you can't fall if you don't trust the other person with your heart. Be open always. You can't expect him to open up to you when you won't open up to him. It is a give and take relationship, when you want to unlock the part of his heart he holds dearest to him.

To make him feel emotionally safe, you have to let him know that you won't let him down. This often means listening to him talk about things you aren't necessarily interested in.

A man has to be able to cry around you to feel truly and completely safe in a relationship. Sometimes you have to assure him that it is okay to cry. Hold him when you see him having a weak moment, and let him know that sometimes even the strongest mountain breaks down. If he can't cry around you, he won't be truly open to you. Men are at their most vulnerable moments in life when they break down in front of someone, because they are bred to believe that crying means you are weak. So if a man finally cries in front of you, you have won his heart.

Here is a scenario of how to know if you make him feel emotionally safe.

Scenario

Josh loved his boyfriend very much, but he felt as if Alex was still closed off. Josh was definitely the more feminine of the two, so he was very open with Alex. Alex however, often changed the subject when it came to his past. Josh knew that Alex loved him, he just wasn't ready to completely open up. Josh was understanding, and never pushed, but still let his love know that he was there for him.

One day, Alex came home in a horrible mood. Josh didn't know what was wrong, but he ran up and hugged Alex anyway.

"Oh, baby, I can just tell you had a horrible day. Would you like to talk about it?" Josh asked.

"Actually I would like that very much, babe." Alex said with a tight throat.

"Come sit down darling, let me make you your favorite tea while you compose your thoughts."

Josh hurried off to the kitchen, while Alex sat down on the couch, looking lost and forlorn. Josh's hear broke just looking at how sad his love looked. After the tea finished brewing, Josh hurried back into the living room, and handed Alex his tea, made just the way he liked it.

"What happened love?" Josh asked gently.

"I guess there is no sense in beating around the bush. My brother is dead. He was shot in the head last night in a drug deal gone wrong." Alex said

"I am so sorry love. I didn't know you had a brother, but I am heartbroken for you nonetheless." Josh said, wrapping his arms around Alex.

"I didn't talk about him much because I was ashamed of him. He was a drug addict. He was always asking when he could meet you, and I always made excuses. I feel horrible now, because he was the only one who supported me when I came out as gay. My parents kicked me out, and he gave me a place to stay. He was the only family I had, and I judged him for something he had about as much control over as I do being gay." Alex broke down in tears.

Josh sat there and held Alex, his heart breaking for him, as it also beamed with love, because Alex was finally opening up to him. He was sad that Alex's only true family was dead, but happy that Alex trusted him enough to tell him everything. His heart swelled with love for the man in his arms crying his eyes out.

Discussion

Alex was very closed off when it came to talking about his past, because it hurt to much to talk about, and he didn't want to cry in front of Josh, and Josh felt distanced from Alex due to his wall he threw up. Once Alex finally started talking about himself, Josh knew that Alex truly loved him, and that he trusted him finally. This gave Josh a happy feeling, even in the midst of a sad time, which allowed him to truly comfort Alex in his moment of need.

Why Do You Need This Key Again?

This key is essential in opening up an intense bond between you and your partner. When you feel comfortable enough to be completely open with each other, you learn more about the other than you could ever imagine. This is important, because to truly love someone, you have to truly know them. Once you truly know everything about someone, loving them becomes a whole lot easier.

Chapter 4:

Secret Key #3

Respect and Compassion

What is the one thing that anyone wants more than anything in the world? That is right, respect. Respect is rated the number one thing that a person wants in life. It is even more of a priority than love, because you can't have love if you don't have respect.

Respect is what makes the world go round. Think Aretha Franklin. R-E-S-P-E-C-T. This song is about how just a little respect can make a world of difference. You have to respect your partner not only as your partner, but as a human being as well. You can't expect them to be perfect, and you have to respect that sometimes they have to make mistakes.

This is where compassion comes in. When your partner makes a mistake, it is always important to show them compassion and understanding. This way they know that you care enough to help them make it through the mistakes they have made.

Why is this a Secret Key?

Most people do not know that men need more respect and compassion in the relationship. Men are often more insecure then women, they are just better at hiding it. Respect and compassion assure him that you love him and care about him, and that he is good enough for you. If he feels that he is worthy of you, he will become the most devoted person you have ever met. This key unlocks the section in his heart tied to fidelity. If he feels worthy of you, he will do anything to stay there. If he does not feel worthy of you, he will look for someone who makes him feel worthy.

EGO

This all boils down to ego. A man's ego is a powerful thing. Sometimes, if not treated properly, he can become borderline narcissistic. If he feels that he is not getting the respect he deserves, he will look to get it in any way he can. This is where a lot of severe relationship problems stem from. Emotional abuse, physical abuse, infidelity. This is all a problem created when a man is beaten down. Not necessarily by you but by the world. This is what causes people to split up, and can ruin what seemed to be a perfect relationship.

Men aren't always aware of their ego issues, so they can't tell you what they need. That is not to excuse a man who becomes abusive or a cheater, or even to say that a man is helpless. They know right from wrong, they just don't realize what is causing them to do wrong. If he is abusive or a cheater, then you should leave. No questions asked. Leave However, if he is just being angry for no reason, maybe you aren't showing each other enough respect and compassion.

How to Show Him Respect

- Be there for him: If he has a gig, or something important, go with him. Even if you aren't interested. Being there for him, and respecting him enough to support him shows him how much you care. If he needs you to listen to him, do so. Let him rant on about something you don't care about, but pay attention. Just because you don't care doesn't give you a free pass to ignore him or tune him out.

- Respect His Privacy: Trust is a big thing in a relationship. Both parties need their privacy on some things, and breaking that privacy is saying that you don't trust your partner enough to give him space. A big thing that a lot of women do is go through his phone. If you can't trust him enough to leave his phone alone, you probably shouldn't be in a relationship. You also shouldn't snoop through his drawers or his personal things. Let him have his privacy, just as you want yours.

- Respect His Personal Space: You don't have to be together every free moment you both have. Sometimes, spending time apart when you have free time is a good thing. You can do your own thing, and don't have to worry about if the other person is having fun. Men need this personal space to unwind after a hard day. Women do as well, but we are focusing on men here. If he doesn't text you back immediately, he is probably in the shower or taking a nice hot bubble bath. It does NOT mean he is cheating on you. Let him have his space without worrying about him stepping out on you. If you trust and respect him, he most likely will not want to do anything to break that trust. But if you don't trust him, he might just give you a reason not to.

- Respect the Fact that He is Human: Men are not robots, and they are not slaves. He has needs, and he needs them tended to at times as well. You cannot expect him to wait on you hand and foot, yet not turn around to do the same for him. Also he will mess up. Don't hang it over his head for the rest of his life. Get through it, and then get over it.

Those are some ways that you can show that you respect him. Men are easy to please, and as they do not have the hormone fluxes that women do, it is more straightforward, but you still have to dig a little to find out his needs. He will give you what you need, if you respect him enough to let him.

Compassion

Compassion is important for when he is having a hard day or makes a mistake. You have to be willing to be compassionate towards someone to ever make a relationship work. Compassion is the difference between healing his heart and breaking it. If you are compassionate, he will trust you with things he doesn't trust anyone else with.

How to Be Compassionate

- Take Care of Him: If he is having a bad day, cook for him. Clean for him. Rub his back and cuddle him. I know this new-age mentality is that women are not a man's slave and that he can do for himself. That may be true, but sometimes you have to take care of him. In return, he will take care of you.

- Be Understanding: Men are human, and they will mess up. Don't overreact if he buys they wrong type of toilet paper, or the wrong grade of milk. They don't always get everything right. You have probably messed up sometimes as well. Did he freak out over the little things? Relax. If he isn't out killing people, or cheating on you, then discuss it calmly on why you prefer things a different way, and then make like Elsa and 'Let it Go'.

- Don't Ridicule Him: If he is not as advanced as you in some areas, do not make him feel bad for it. If you can read the best, and he can do math the best, combine your strengths. Don't make him feel like less of a person because he can't do what you can. Don't tell him he needs to get better. If he wants to, then help him, but don't tell him he has to.

- Listen to His Problems: The best thing you can ever do is just listen when he wants to talk. Not only will you learn some new things, but you will show him that you are invested in him, and by showing him a little compassion, you make him feel like he is important.

This scenario will show you how respect and compassion can help save a relationship.

Scenario

Rachel was worried about Rick. He had been acting distant lately, and was gone a lot. He always hid his phone and wouldn't let her touch it. Everyone said that he was probably cheating, but she trusted him to have a good reason for all of these things. She didn't want to be let down again by another man.

I will have a talk with him when he gets home tonight. I will ask him why he has been acting this way.

Suddenly she heard a phone ring. She checked her pockets, but it wasn't hers. She investigated the sound, and found her boyfriend's phone behind the toilet. There was a strange number calling.

Should I answer it? No. I trust him. It is probably just a telemarketer, and his phone probably fell behind the toilet this morning, and he didn't grab it cause he was running late to work.

Rachel knew that Rick would be home in a few hours, so she busied herself with errands and cleaning the house up. Five o'clock rolled by, and Rick still wasn't home. She started to get worried, and with no way to contact him, she couldn't allay her fears. But she told herself to remain calm, and that he would show up.

Finally, around seven o'clock, Rick came walking in the door. Rachel flung herself into his arms because she was so worried. Then she noticed that he didn't smell like the fiberglass mill, and he was surprisingly clean for being at work all day.

"Rick. We really need to talk." Rachel whispered, on the verge of tears.

"What's wrong?" Rick asked her

"I have been trusting of you, and I still trust you to tell me what is going on. I am trying not to assume you are cheating. However it is really hard to think of any other explanation why you have been coming home late, hiding your phone behind the toilet and getting strange calls. I didn't answer it by the way. Your clothes are too clean to be coming out of the fiberglass company, and they are the same clothes you walked out of here wearing. You don't smell like you normally do after work. Please just tell me what is going on." Rachel burst into tears.

"Oh Rach." Rick sighed, pulling her into his arms. "I got laid off a couple of weeks ago, and have been looking for a job ever since. That number was probably a job calling so I have to call back tomorrow. I'm late because I have been doing odd jobs to continue making enough money to support us, so you don't have to. I wanted to tell you, I just didn't want you to worry."

"That is what this is all about? You knew I was cheated on several times by my last guy, and you leave me worrying that it is happening again? Babe, I would have understood if you had told me, and I would have supported you, and even got a job myself if need be. I love you, and I want you to tell me about your problems. Please don't hide something like this again."

"Oh Rachel, I love you so much, and I didn't realize how bad it looked. I am so sorry, and I promise to always tell you about these things from now on." Rick said, kissing Rachel passionately.

Discussion

Rachel could have jumped to conclusions and accused Rick of cheating on her, thus making him angry for her not trusting him. However, she decided to ask him about it and listen to what he had to say. She was understanding when he told her what was going on, and let him know she wanted him to bring his troubles to her, even if it meant that he had to put some stress on her. She wanted to take on these problems together.

By being compassionate, and respecting him enough to trust him, she avoided what could have been a really big fight. Instead they were brought closer together, as they opened up with what was bothering them.

Why is this Key Important Again?

You have to respect each other to get anywhere in a relationship. Without respect you have nothing, and you can't truly love someone if you do not respect them. Compassion is needed to ensure that your relationship is not a miserable one. You have to respond with compassion to avoid having an argument blown out of proportion. People are not robots or dolls, they will mess up.

You have to use this key to unlock the part of a man's heart that trusts you. He doesn't open it up for just anyone. Most men do not trust half of the people they say are close to them. They could not be vulerable to these people. You have to unlock that for yourself.

Chapter 5:

Secret Key #3

Be Confident

Men do not want to be with a woman who is always questioning if she is good enough for him. They want a woman who knows her worth. Men want to know they are with someone who feels valued. If you aren't confident, it makes his job of making you feel secure that much harder. He feels he always has to lift your self esteem, and that can be a hard job for anyone.

Confidence is not always just knowing you are worthy of love, however. It is also taking care of yourself. Taking care of your personal hygiene and keeping yourself groomed. You do not have to be perfect, just put an effort into keeping yourself clean and well kept.

Most people don't realize that this is important in a relationship, and that is what makes it a secret key. It is important to use this to unlock his desires for you if you are looking to start a relationship with him, and you must remain confident and well kept to unlock his never waning desires for you.

Confidence

Everyone has their insecurities, there is no doubt about that. However it is important to not let your insecurities rule your life. You can have some things that make you not so sure about yourself, but you have to be able to work through them.

Confidence is important in any aspect of your life, but it is certainly important in relationships. Not only do you have to be confident in yourself, you have to be confident in your relationship as well. You can't expect a relationship to thrive if you don't have any confidence in it. You have to believe that it will succeed, and that you are good enough for it to succeed.

In this scenario, you will learn more about what poor confidence can do to a relationship.

Scenario

Blake was super insecure. He constantly doubted himself, and if he was good enough for his boyfriend Michael. Michael hated that Blake was so insecure, and wished he could see how gorgeous he was. It caused many fights, because Blake felt that he wasn't good enough and did everything in his power to make Michael see that. Which included picking fights for no reason at all.

I wish I was confident enough to make this relationship work. I am just not good enough for him. He is perfect, and I am a fat lard. I really need to lose weight. I am so fat. Why does he stay with me? Can't he see I'm a disaster?

These are the thoughts that went through Blake's head daily. He couldn't ever get close to Michael, because he was scared that Michael would see that he was a disaster. He constantly had a wall up that Michael was trying to break down.

I'm exhausted. Blake never lets me in, and I'm am so tired of trying to break through the walls he puts up. I wish he could see how much he means to me. He is perfect just the way he is, if only he would stop worrying so much.

Michael was tired of always trying to boost Blake's self esteem, so with a heavy heart, he broke up with Blake.

"I told you I wasn't good enough!" Blake screamed, with tears in his eyes.

"You imbecile! That is the reason I am breaking up with you! You don't feel like you are good enough for me, and I am tired of you ignoring every effort I make to try to show you otherwise! You are perfect just the way you are, and I wish I could have made you see that! I don't want to leave, but I can't keep breaking my heart when you won't let me into yours!" Michael yelled back.

"So you aren't breaking up with me because I'm not breaking up with you, you are merely breaking up with me because I feel like I am not?" Blake whispered

"Yes. I want nothing more than to be with you, but I have to think of my own emotional health as well."

"What if I promised to get help for my insecurities? Would you stay with me? I love you Michael, I just don't want to be hurt anymore. I want you to love me too."

"I do love you Blake, and if you actively get help, then yes, I will stay. But you have two weeks to show me you are trying." Michael said, embracing Blake.

Discussion

Blake's insecurities almost cost him the love of his life. He was so worried about Michael pushing him away, that he didn't realize he was the one doing the pushing. Blake was not confident in himself, and it was tiresome for Michael to always be the one to supply the confidence for the both of them. Michael felt like Blake couldn't truly love him, because he never let him in. It almost destroyed their relationship beyond repair.

If Blake had realized that Michael wanted to be with him for who he was, he would have avoided this whole scene, and been very happy. Let your confidence shine through. You may not feel confident, but fake it until you make it. If you seem confident, you will start to feel confident.

Take Care of Yourself

Men want women to be healthy. This does not mean that you have to eat organic food, and wear full face makeup every day of your life. Just shower regularly, and keep yourself groomed. If you are a slob, and unhygienic, most men will feel that is a sign of lack of confidence, and they will stay away from you. You have to make yourself appear to be ready for a relationship to find the right relationship. If you look like you don't care about yourself you are going to attract someone who doesn't care about you as well.

If you are in a relationship, and start letting yourself go, you will make your man feel like you don't care about the relationship as much as you used to. (This doesn't count if you have kids. Though you should still try to shower regularly) You should always want to keep your hygiene up regardless of your relationship status.

Why is this Key Important?

This key unlocks a man's desire for you. Human's primal instinct is to mate, and men are really close to their primal instincts. He will be looking for a strong woman suitable for carrying his children, so that his offspring are strong and successful. By being confident, and taking care of yourself, you attract men that will value you, and treat you well. If you are not confident, and do not take care of yourself, you often will attract losers and abusers.

Chapter 6:

Secret Key #5

Give and Take on the Lead

This key is one of the most secret keys there are, because most people don't realize that the man doesn't always wear the pants in a relationship. You both have to make the big decisions together, and take turns on the smaller ones. You cannot let one single person take control of the relationship. If you work together, you unlock a bond that allows him to see you as an equal and not as below him.

If you make all of the decisions in the relationship, you allow him to be passive, but if he makes all the decisions, you become passive. Neither one of you should become passive, because this is a one way ticket to a controlling relationship. While it does not always end up that way, fifty six percent of relationships where one person is in charge of most or all of the decisions turn into be abusive relationships.

The solution to avoid this problem is to take turns making decisions. Even the smaller decisions like where to go when you go out to eat, or what to watch on television. On the bigger decisions, make them together. Especially on whether or not to buy a house or start a family, or any big purchase.

Also, take care of finances together, or split them up equally. You cannot give one person complete control of the finances, and expect to not have some control issues. Money is the biggest player in a controlling relationship. If one person has all the control of the money, they can tell the other partner what they can and cannot do, and once you get a taste of that power, it escalates from there.

The best way to avoid this is to get a joint account if you are married that has both of your names on it, so you both can access the funds, or have separate accounts with only your name on it, so the other partner can't access the funds. If you do this though, you have to decide how to split the bills. Otherwise, there will be issues with bills not getting paid, and utilities being shut off. This is if you live together. If not, you don't have to worry about it.

If you don't want to take turns on even the little decisions, then work together to decide everything. From where you want to eat, to where you want to live. Working together will create a strong bond between you two as well. You will grow closer together as you achieve things together. Think about it. If you make great strides in your life with the one you love, who are you going to celebrate with? That's right, them. So it only makes sense that if you make all your decisions together, you will grow closer due to the fact that you celebrate every achievement as one. You have to want to work together though, otherwise, you will argue more than you work together.

Why is this Key Important?

You want to unlock his heart in a way that makes him see you as an equal rather than a lesser, as society tries to make everyone think. If he sees you as his equal, he will learn to depend on you, rather than walk all over you. There will be less debates on who should make what decisions, and who is always right, because you will both be able to compromise and work together to achieve a blissful relationship.

PART VIII

CHAPTER 1

WHAT DO YOU WANT?

Do you walk into an electronics store or a car dealership without knowing what you want? No, if you are like most men, you buy magazines that tell you all the technical specs about the latest technology and cars. You also go online to forums and tech websites to do research.

Why would you try to pick up women or try dating sites without knowing what you want? You do not want to do that. If you are like most men, then you have dated, enjoyed one-night stands, and explored the pool of women.

Now, you are reading this book because you are looking for something more. Perhaps, you haven't dated more than a few women and wonder what you are doing wrong?

The men who are successful in relationships, who find those long term marriages—they are the ones who know what they want.

I'll give you an example of a marriage that lasted 42 years. It would have lasted longer if illness did not exist. This couple met when the wife moved into a new apartment complex with two other female friends. The young man, at the time, came up to see if there was anyone he wanted to date or would want to go on dates with him.

He would call up the night he wanted to date and see if someone was willing. He even spent eight months in another state. But, this man realized he had met the one person for him in that apartment.

He came back from living in a different place with one thing in mind— to ensure this woman would date him. He tried his nonchalant style, calling up the day of to ask for a date. She would always refuse because she also had other plans already in the works.

Finally, this man asked, "what do I have to do to get you to go out with me?"

The answer was simple, "call in advance."

The couple dated a few times before Christmas, every week during January and were engaged the day before Valentines.

Life doesn't always happen this way, but you can be sure that the man knew what he wanted. He dated several women, going out when they were available, and enjoying coffee, a meal, or a movie. But, no one caught his attention as much as the woman he married. It took distance to realize that no other woman compared.

If you have not dated very many people, then you need to get out there. You need to start dating more. How else are you supposed to figure out what you want?

I'll give you another example. This couple was together for 17 years and married for 13, almost 14 years. The marriage ended with a divorce and two suffering children. The man dated only two people, marrying the second. The woman had dated more men, but also enjoyed being the center of attention, the person that knows it all, and the person who lies because she doesn't recognize the truth. When the husband asked her father for her hand, the father said, "she is just like her mother, are you sure you know what you are doing?" Her mother constantly spends every dime that is earned, is all about herself, and often depressed and unhappy. Of course, the husband thought he could live with it all, only to find that the woman he was marrying could easily ask for a divorce and immediately move in with another man.

The lesson in this second example is—you can know what you want and what you are capable of living with, but you also have to make allowances for the other person.

A person who cannot love themselves will never be able to love another with their whole heart.

Are you willing to accept being second or loved with less than a whole heart? Are you willing to date or marry someone when, you know, eventually, it will come to an end, it's just a matter of how long it takes? These are the questions you need to ask yourself as you begin to learn the secrets to enter a woman's heart completely. Only when you know yourself and what you are willing to accept, can you truly find your way into the right woman's heart.

CHAPTER 2

SECRET KEY #1

Open, Honest, Consistent Communication

Pick up a woman's magazine that has a quiz. I bet that quiz has a section on communication. It probably tests the woman on how communicative her partner is and offers advice on how to elicit more communication. There are millions of these quizzes and articles in magazines, online, and they are all designed for woman by woman. Yet, you can learn something from this concept. Why do you think communication is such a hot topic? It is because women are fundamentally different from men.

Women can be extremely intuitive, even read body language, bu women still consider the way men think a mystery. Women canno believe a man is only thinking about sex. There has to be something more in your brains, right? You are capable of multitasking at your job of dating multiple women, and holding deep conversations on politics religion, engineering or something equally complicated—so you mus have more on your mind than sex.

You also have feelings. These feelings can be hurt. You can also be excited and feel love. Women are unable to understand why you are unable to talk about these deeper feelings, and demand that you do.

A group of women get together and they catch up. What has happened in your life, what are you doing now, what happened last week. The conversation invariably turns to emotions, but it is not the whole discussion.

Women seek other women for emotional support and understanding because they feel they lack it from the men in their life. Women also work on hormones more so than men.

It's a fact and not something you should fear discussing. A woman can be happy one moment and the wrong words can flip a switch. The grudge can be held for days with the wrong words. A man usually forgets about the issue in a few hours or days, unless the same thing keeps happening.

So, on one hand, women have a need to know your emotions because they cannot understand them unless you tell them. On the other, there are emotional mind fields that you have to navigate as you communicate.

It has been the experience of most women that men do not want to communicate about their feelings. They find it a waste of time. Yet, it is the one thing that will help your woman feel confident in the relationship. It is the way for you to work your way into their heart. The key is for this communication to be open, honest and consistent.

Defining Open

What does open communication mean? In business, it is a setting where employees are encouraged to share their thoughts and concerns, without the fear of retaliation (reference.com). In a relationship, it is the same thing, only the thoughts and concerns to be shared are about personal situations.

Communication includes issues about one's job, the treatment of the person by their boss, monetary concerns, kids, religion, love, and all other feelings people have.

For example, a family of four sat around a dinner table to discuss whether a move to a new state would be the best option for their family. The discussion included the changes that would occur, the employment options for the parents, and why the move would offer monetary stability versus the current place they lived. Each person was given a chance to discuss their thoughts, fears, concerns, and acceptance of the move.

Another family of four also moved. In this family, the parents sat their children down, said they were moving, and stated where. No communication from the children was allowed as to how they felt or why a move had to occur.

Do you think the children in the first family were more prepared and less unsettled than the second family? Of course, they were. They weighed in with their opinion, fears, concerns, and desires. The second family's children had to keep what they thought to themselves.

Now, consider this example, as a communication between two people: You have two people in a relationship, where one person is always stating what is going to happen, without giving reasons or why it is the best? How unsettled will the partner be? How angry do you think they will become at not having a choice?

Open communication is required to help your woman understand how you think, the reasons behind your actions, and to feel secure in the relationship. If you do not share your thoughts and feelings, how are they to know what you are really thinking? How are they to feel secure that you truly care about them, if they are not kept in the loop or considered part of the equation.

The game telephone provides a good example of this concept. One person starts a statement and by the end of ten or twenty people the statement has changed drastically. By the time your body signals based on your emotions are translated by a woman, they are changed because she is going to interpret them based on how she thinks, just like you try to interpret her behavior based on how you think.

Without communication, you are unable to figure out what each of you is thinking.

Honest Communication

Does this outfit make me look fat? Yes. Ouch. But, it is also how you deliver the answer. You need to be honest because there is one thing a woman does not want—she doesn't want to wear something that does not look good and she will feel embarrassed about later on. Also, here is the kicker—if you lie about how she looks in an outfit—what else could you be lying about?

It is far better to tell the truth when asked for it, then to lie. Furthermore, it is 100% better to speak the truth in any situation. If there is a behavior that bothers you, speak up. One woman told her husband this, "If I start acting like my mother, tell me." She was fearful that she would start displaying certain negative behavior that her mother had and she didn't want to. She was always hurt when being told "you are acting like your mother," but it also helped her realize that a correction to her behavior was required.

A woman who loves herself and gives of herself, completely, to the man she loves is capable of accepting the truth. The anger and stewing for a few hours is better than ignoring the problem or lying to avoid conflict.

Now will all women agree, no. Some women are unable to take the hurt that honest communication provides, but ask yourself, do you want a woman who can give her whole heart because she values your honesty or the woman who keeps a grudge and eventually causes too much pain?

You want the woman who can give her whole heart, so be honest in your communication and explain why you will always tell the truth, even if it is not what the person wants to hear. You'll be valued for this behavior because you are noticing and trying, as well as remaining truthful.

Consistency

More times than I have fingers I have seen relationships start where each person is honest, and communicative. However, after a year or two, the communication stops being consistent. It is like each man and woman believe they have figured the person out and know what they are thinking, so it is less necessary to be communicative. Wrong.

You cannot become complacent just because it seems like the woman is not demanding communication as often as she was. There are only a few reasons she feels communication is no longer as necessary:

- She thinks she knows you well enough that she can read your moods.

- She is no longer interested.

- She is angry when you don't truly communicate.

If it is the first, then you need to show her that talking each night before you go to sleep is important to you. You need to give of yourself for her to continue giving of herself.

If she is no longer interested, you need to know, so you can move on to find the right person. Sometimes a woman has just as much difficulty breaking off a relationship. She doesn't want to cause hurt when she is unwilling to give her whole heart.

The last reason is fairly easy to discern. If you have not provided any worthwhile communication, then she will turn away, say "fine whatever," or something along those words and stop trying to communicate with you.

For communication to unlock your woman's heart, you need to:

- Learn to read body language

- Read the subtle nuances in her tone

- And give of yourself before you ask her to give of herself

If you are embarrassed about your thoughts because they are just about "sex" in that moment—don't be. Tell her. But more than anything, have a time of day when the two of you talk about what happened at work, the challenges or the good things, and plans that you have on things that you want to do.

The conversation does not have to be deep and always about emotions each night. Rather, you are supposed to come together, be honest, be consistent, and just share. You are not to judge, just to listen, with attentiveness. If you only hear the words, then you cannot repeat them. Here is something else that is usually a complaint from a guy, "all she has ever said are complaints. We never talk about anything other than how much she hates this or that."

Did you ever think that perhaps she is not happy with something that could be changed? Perhaps she needs a new perspective? Maybe, feelings of unhappiness in other areas of her life are making her complain about something else? The biggest one—did you ever think that she only communicates when there is something negative?

Try it, if you are already in a relationship. Track your communication for a week. Did your woman want to talk when she was happy or did she only want to talk when something was bothering her? Did you try to get her to talk about her day or the happy stuff, or did you think "yay, I don't have to try communicating today?"

Your effort to get her to talk when she is happy, will be rewarded. She will know that she can talk about anything, but more that you care to listen about everything. She will learn to talk about the good and the bad, so you don't hear only the unhappy things.

Thus, the ultimate secret is your effort in getting her to communicate about all things, just as much as she is asking you to communicate about anything at all.

One man said, "I didn't think you wanted to listen. I figured it would bore you."

His statement was definitely an insight into why he lacked communication. It was also the key his partner needed to understand that she needed to put more effort into listening.

Most try to say that communication is a two-way street, but is it really? If you drive on a two-way street, you have to keep to your own lane to avoid an accident. I suppose you could "meet in the middle," and block traffic. I'd rather think of communication as a one-way street. One of you has to be illegally driving to meet in the middle, but sometimes that is what it takes for a heart to open. If you are not willing to put in the effort to circumvent any blocks in the way, such as illegally driving down a one-way street, then how can you open up her heart?

She will see the motivation and honesty in your effort to communicate on all subjects that are important to you and her, not just what may be important to her. This will open her heart a little further, and allow her to trust in your feelings for her.

CHAPTER 3

SECRET KEY #2

Equality and Respect

This is a chapter that should be common sense, but more often than not, it is not. Countries were founded on inequality and there are many still struggling with inequality issues to the point that women are killed if they step out of line. Given how sensitive a topic this is—it should not surprise you that all women want to be treated equally and with respect.

Yes, there are people with more intellect than others, but talking down to them or disrespecting them is not the proper way to communicate. What if you were faced with a woman who had an IQ of 185 and she consistently talked down to you even about simple topics? A man's pride gets pricked pretty easy. It is annoying when a woman is or acts smarter than you. So, why wouldn't it be annoying and insensitive if you are always acting smarter than the woman you are with.

Here is an example: A young man not very well versed in subtle body language and common sense would talk about simple things, a topic that he had in common with a young woman. But, he would often use an arrogant tone with an "I know more than you" attitude. He would tell this young woman things she already knew, like she didn't know the first thing about it.

The relationship didn't last. Nor will any relationship in this situation, when the woman is capable of knowing herself, her own intellect, and a proper way of having a conversation.

It doesn't have to always be about conversation, either. It is just an easy example that helps shore up the previous chapter.

When you communicate in a relationship, the woman wants to be seen as your equal, to have an equal opinion. She doesn't want her words discounted because you know better.

She wants her words to resonate, for you to think about them, and help explain why something else would be better or why her opinion is valued, but not the right approach.

For example, let's say you are married and you have a child. Your child starts to refuse to eat. You might have a different viewpoint than your wife. Your wife might allow the child to go to bed without food until the child finally figures out that starving is not the answer. You might not want your child to go to bed hungry, so you will allow your child to choose a healthy snack such as apples and cheese.

Your wife feels that you are giving in to your child and their refusal to eat healthy things. You might feel that letting your child go hungry, can have unhealthy consequences. Who is right or wrong? That is not the answer. The question is who is going to see results quicker? If the father will get the child to eat healthy foods, then the child will remain healthy. If the child continues to not eat enough, even with healthy snacks then this can hinder the path to a solution. Whereas, starving often gets a child to eat, even a little of something they don't like or a willingness to try it cooked a different way in order to never go to bed hungry again.

The debate won't be answered here because the point is not to solve the question, but to realize that if you refuse to listen to your partner's opinion, harm could be done in more ways than one. You could end up hurting your child and on the other hand, you are putting your wife in a position of disrespect in front of the child.

Dismissing what your partner, whether you are dating, going to the next step, or married, is not going to get her to open her heart to you. Are you always right 100% of the time in all areas? Of course not, and neither is your partner.

The key is for you two to be able to see each other as equals. You look at each other, know your strengths and weaknesses, and compromise when necessary, but never with a disrespectful attitude.

It is okay to point out certain mistakes, but make sure you do it with respect. Value the person and they will open their heart to you. They will also value you more, for showing that you value them.

If you have not yet noticed this is leading to "trust." For a woman to give their entire heart to you—they need to trust you, trust that you understand them, respect them, and value what they have to say or to give in the relationship.

Communication is not the only way to make this known. Body language is also very important in a woman being seen as an equal. If you ignore something they say or do, it is an act of disrespect, of seeing them as less.

For you it may be complacency. You might be used to the person always cooking your dinner, so you forget to say thank you or take notice of their hard work. The husband or boyfriend who is successful never lets anything go unnoticed.

Car Doors and Other Doors

"She has her own hands; she can open the door."

Have you ever thought this? Perhaps you know someone who has? Maybe, the women you have dated told you it is unnecessary to open doors for her?

Yes, a woman likes to do for herself, but that doesn't mean you should never open a door for her. Choose your moments. Make it a surprise. Even a woman who is capable and willing to open her own doors, appreciates when a gentleman will do it for her. It is based on when you open the door.

For instance, let's say your girlfriend has her arms full of things and there is no hand to open the door. You would immediately open it for her, right? Of course.

The next time you need to open the door is when you are taking her out for a special dinner.

"Let me get the door." This statement tells her that you appreciate that she is coming with you and that she has dressed lovely for the evening. It is a "special" occasion that supersedes the usual rule that she will open her own doors.

If you are running late and it is easier for your partner to open her door, then wait and she doesn't mind opening her own door—it is okay to let her. If she is the type that always needs the door open as a sign of chivalry, then you still, have to open it.

It is not about the door. It is about the effort and respect such an action provides. Again, you let the woman make a choice based on her preferences or you simply ask what she prefers. You choose your moments to be sweet or you always show respect because that is what your heart tells you to do.

There are men who will tell a woman, "I was raised to open doors as a sign of respect. Not complying with this, goes against the respect I have for you."

The key again is to communicate what you know to be right, so that your partner also understands your point of view.

You should back down to show your respect, but also in the same light tell her that you are respecting her more by following through with certain instincts.

Remember these suggestions are examples. You have your upbringing and your partner will have hers. As long as you show mutual respect for each other, and equality of the minds, then you will have a woman who is willing to show you her heart.

CHAPTER 4

SECRET KEY #3

Acceptance for Who They Are

What is the one thing many women have tried to do when they started dating you? They tried to change you. The wrong woman always tries to change her partner. They want you to fit into an ideal they have for a man. There are plenty of reasons for this.

- She is afraid of never finding someone who will accept her

- She feels you are broken and in need of fixing

The two bullet points are the two main reasons she may try to change you. A smart woman will eventually realize that she cannot change the man she is dating. She has to accept him for who he is, his faults and strengths, or find someone else.

You may wish to change the woman you are dating too. Perhaps she doesn't care enough about her appearance? Maybe, she shops and spends too much money? It may be something simple that you do not like, but cannot seem to ignore.

You have an option. You can stop dating a person because she has habits or traits you cannot ignore or you can accept them. It is your choice, but you need to make it.

Don't stay with someone because of your own fear. Yes, men do have fears. There are men out there who fear that they will have to settle for one woman because the one they want is unattainable. Did you ever think that you are not settling, but finding the person who is right for you? Do not settle if things do not feel right and in the same vain do not choose a woman who you cannot accept for her faults and strengths.

If you already have problems or fights due to basic personality clashes, then you are not going to get the woman to stay with you and give her full heart.

The secret is to truly accept, no matter what or to realize that you cannot. If you can accept all of her faults, then you will open her heart a little more, and eventually her whole heart will be yours.

The one thing you cannot do is change your mind and expect her to open her heart. She has to know that there is consistency within your own heart. You either accept her for who she is or you don't. If you do not really accept her faults, then you will always have doubts in your mind. You will always question or find yourself focusing on the things you cannot accept.

People can only change themselves if they see a problem. They are not going to change because you want the change to happen. For a time, they may try to be better, but after a while, their inherent traits will win out. There is no way around the traits winning, unless the person they are a part of is willing to change.

Yes, you received an example earlier that stated the wife wanted to know when she was acting like her mother. The key here is that she wanted to know. She asked for the truth. She was already in the frame of mind that she may need to change her behavior if she became like her mother.

If you try to point out things to a woman who has not asked or does not think there is something wrong within herself, then you are not going to succeed. She will close her heart and doubt that you can love her fully when you cannot accept all of who she is.

There is also a difference in accepting who a woman is and being her support for the changes that she wishes to make.

What if the woman you are dating had a bad family experience as a child? What if she lacks confidence? Can you deal with her frame of mind and self-doubt? What if you could be her support to help her build her self-confidence without actually pointing out that she needs the help?

It is possible. If you are open and willing to accept the woman for who she is and the potential of who she desires to be, then you are going to find her whole heart is in your hands.

By now you should see a theme in the secrets to a woman's heart: trust and support.

Any woman you date needs to feel they can trust you and that you will be supportive. Without trust and support, she is going to feel like you are only partially in the relationship and she is going to hold back.

It does not matter how many relationships you have had that reach the next level from dating casually to steadily. It does not matter if you have married before and your marriage has failed or is struggling. If you can provide trust and support for the woman you value in your life, you will finally succeed in opening her complete heart to you.

The Pedestal

One man succeeded and another did not. There was a time when one woman was dating two men. She would go out on Fridays with one guy and Saturdays with the other. Both men knew she was dating someone else, but they had never met. One man asked for her hand and was given a "yes." The other took her to a wrestling match the day she received the marriage proposal. The next date he found out she was going to marry the other guy and asked, "are you sure. I love you, you are everything to me, I've put you on a pedestal and don't know how I can live without you being my wife."

The woman's answer: "Your first mistake was putting me on a pedestal."

No one wants to be on a pedestal.

Already it was mentioned that you need to accept the woman for who she is. A part of this discussion is about that very concept. You do need to accept a woman's faults.

More importantly, you cannot raise a woman too higher than she truly is. You cannot have a "celebrity" image of the woman you wish to date.

What if every woman went around trying to find her perfect guy from the romance novels she reads or the songs that have been sung?
You know she won't find this guy because you know men have faults and are not romantic heroes like in the books and movies.
You cannot put a woman on a pedestal and expect a life of happiness to follow.
The minute you put a woman on a pedestal is the minute your relationship is wrong.
You have to be supportive and help her learn to trust you, but you cannot make her a "goddess," in your mind.
Do not keep the rose colored glasses on and reference what you truly want.
What do you wish to see in a woman you can spend your life with? Are you the type of man who needs space, but will never stray? Can you look at attractive women, but know that the one beside you, is the most attractive because of the entire package? If so, then you don't need a pedestal for her. You just need to marry her if you haven't already.

CHAPTER 5

SECRET KEY #4

The Pedestal

One man succeeded and another did not. There was a time when one woman was dating two men. She would go out on Fridays with one guy and Saturdays with the other. Both men knew she was dating someone else, but they had never met. One man asked for her hand and was given a "yes." The other took her to a wrestling match the day she received the marriage proposal. The next date he found out she was going to marry the other guy and asked, "are you sure. I love you, you are everything to me, I've put you on a pedestal and don't know how I can live without you being my wife."

The woman's answer: "Your first mistake was putting me on a pedestal."

No one wants to be on a pedestal.

Already it was mentioned that you need to accept the woman for who she is. A part of this discussion is about that very concept. You do need to accept a woman's faults.

More importantly, you cannot raise a woman too higher than she truly is. You cannot have a "celebrity" image of the woman you wish to date.

What if every woman went around trying to find her perfect guy from the romance novels she reads or the songs that have been sung?

You know she won't find this guy because you know men have faults and are not romantic heroes like in the books and movies.

You cannot put a woman on a pedestal and expect a life of happiness to follow.

The minute you put a woman on a pedestal is the minute your relationship is wrong.

You have to be supportive and help her learn to trust you, but you cannot make her a "goddess," in your mind.

Do not keep the rose colored glasses on and reference what you truly want.

What do you wish to see in a woman you can spend your life with? Are you the type of man who needs space, but will never stray? Can you look at attractive women, but know that the one beside you, is the most attractive because of the entire package? If so, then you don't need a pedestal for her. You just need to marry her if you haven't already.

CHAPTER 6

SECRET KEY #5

Make Her Smile

The key to most women's hearts is to make her smile and laugh. The right woman will accept your personality, whether it is sarcastic humor or witty humor. It is also the effort you provide in making her smile or laugh. For example, a coworker recently knew his female coworker was having a bad day. They are friends and nothing more, as there is a significant difference in age. Yet, the man, going through his own trials, still worked for a good hour to make her laugh and smile rather than to continue crying as she was doing.

This is a man who understands that humor, even in making silly faces, giving out zinger, witty remarks, is the key to making a woman fall a little in love, even if it is only friendship.

You don't have to be the wittiest. You may have a stupid joke that makes one groan more than laugh or smile. However, the effort in trying to make the woman smile, to make her laugh, will instantly make her heart melt.

Gifts are Important

Surprise gifts are important to a woman. They consider these gifts as supportive or endearing because you are paying attention to her. There are times when life gets routine, mundane, and even filled with complacency on both of your sides. The trick is to come home with a surprise.

Flowers are nice for some women. For others, they are an instant allergy issue. Some men feel that flowers are going to die, so why spend the money, when something else can be provided, such as a vacation from saving money on the little things.

The key is to know what your woman believes and what you can do that will matter to her heart. Sometimes it can be the silliest thing or the simplest. What if you both love tattoos? Did you ever think about getting a tattoo of a symbol or date that matters to both of you?

Perhaps, it is as simple as coming home with a card. Maybe when she goes on a business trip you hide a card in her bag moments before you say goodbye at the airport.

Gifts do not have to be expensive, they do not have to be jewelry, but they do need to be thought of and given. Yes, some women prefer expensive gifts, even demand them, and if you have a wife or partner like this, then you need to comply sometimes. It goes back to accepting and knowing the woman you have in your life. However, it doesn't mean that small things like cards and spontaneous gifts that are not expensive won't move her heart.

It is all about what you know about her desires, what she is used to, and what will make her smile and love you because of the effort you have shown. You can also show a woman used to expensive gifts that it is not the money, but the honesty behind the gift that matters the most.

CHAPTER 7

Special Bonus Tips

Not all women will fit your personality. There are some women who should not be in relationships or marry, unless they can find a partner who is just like them in the key ways. There are even some women who will never open their heart and find true happiness because they cannot find it in themselves. These bonus tips will help you look at relationships and women, so you might succeed, when you have faced certain issues such as being in a bad relationship, failing to be supportive in small ways, or even noticing her each and every day.

Things to Look Out For

- Does your current partner feel love is shown through how much you buy her?

- Does she flirt with other men to see if you are getting angry or noticing what she is doing?

- Does she seem to pick a fight or get angry for no reason you can see?

- Has she started to withdraw from you?

- Is she starting to ignore you, your phone calls, or breaking dates?

These are a few signs that you need to look out for in understanding that she is not the woman for you. Some of these can also be a sign that she may have a psychological issue that she cannot get passed and will eventually affect the relationship.

For instance, have you ever date a woman who lies, who tries to separate you from friends and family, needs "things" to feel you love her, and is always thinking about herself? This can be the sign of a narcissist. A narcissist is someone who views themselves as the most important, cannot handle when someone else is more important, is often arrogant, and knows everything. This same person also blames everyone around them for being at fault and for doing things they are actually doing.

Toxic relationships like this need to be avoided, even if you feel you can live with this person's faults. Drama is another word that has been applied to women who seem to cause conflict, always pick a fight, and have a healthy sexual appetite that never seems satisfied with just one person.

Only you can truly say what type of relationship you are looking for, but there are definitely signs that you need to watch out for with regards to women and drama they can create.

- A woman can call you several times a day or demand that you call them often.

- They may ask where you were and not trust your answer.

- They may text or try to start up a conversation that is too deep on the first meeting.

- They may complain and find nothing happy.

These are just a few other signs that a woman may not be right for you or perhaps anyone. Someone who is obsessive without actually dating you can have psychological issues that require a professional. It may not be nice to say of one's own sex, but it is also the truth. Some women need to recognize their failings and accept those in order to find a healthy relationship, otherwise they are "crazy" in their actions towards men, bordering on obsessive.

Signs of a Wrong Relationship

Relationships do not have to be filled with "crazy" or drama to be wrong for you. There are definite signs that a woman is not right for you, when she is unwilling to give her heart to you. It is not a matter of you trying harder to be supportive, and not complacent in the relationship.

Here is an example of a woman. See if you can see why she might be wrong for a relationship with you.

- She prefers her own company to others.

- She has social anxiety.

- She needs a routine and does not like that routine to be interrupted.

- She is hyper-organized, hating when someone fills up a space she just cleaned.

- She cannot trust easily.

- She is unwilling to be hurt and face the loss of a husband, preferring to die before any of her family, so she doesn't have to face that horrible situation.

- She also has a dislike of touch, something no one can pinpoint a cause for, but one that holds her from a deep physical relationship.

Obviously, this is an extreme example, but take note of it. Sometimes the signs are subtle and other times there is a big sign saying "this is not right." A woman who does not allow physical contact after three dates either has issues with physical contact or does not see you as a sexual partner. A relationship that is not right for you will have fights, ups and downs, and disagreements on the main issues. You won't be able to agree on politics, religion, children, and life in general.

Additional Effort Options

A couple was having trouble in their marriage. The wife was unhappy. The man knew it, but couldn't figure out what to do. He decided he would ask her each morning, "what can I do to make your day better?" At first, his wife thought he was being insensitive and joking. After he kept asking she realized that he meant it and started answering, as well as asking how she could make his day better.

Such a simple phrase and the care behind it saved the marriage. You can do something like this in your relationship. It doesn't have to be a big deal. It can be something as simple as asking how your partner's day was or how you can make it better.

It can also be something that will make her smile. The married couple of 42 years is another great example. One child was grown, married, and nearing having children. The second child left home to live 3,000 miles away. Living as just the two of them, the wife was missing her children. To make her day better, the husband took one of the stuffed animals his daughter left when she moved away, and started creating funny scenes.

One day the orangutan stuffed animal was holding a fake cigarette and reading in their bed. The next day it was playing chess with one of the wife's stuffed bears of similar size. For over a week, the husband would wake up, create a scene, leave for work, and his wife would come home to it. She would smile. Now she has pictures of these scenes to help her memory, since the husband passed away from early onset dementia. These little efforts changed the wife's outlook for the day, the ache in her heart from missing her daughter, and now is a comfort to her with him gone.

What can you think to do that would have such a lasting impact because it is guaranteed to open the woman's heart for life.

Flowers are acceptable, of course, and even desired by most women. But, if you have the imagination, find something that can truly make her smile, laugh, or even cry with happiness. It matters.

Helping Your Partner become a Better Her

The couple who spent 42 years together respected each other, loved each other, and were best friends as well as husband and wife. One of the biggest impacts the husband had on his wife, was mutual respect, equality, and the power to give her what made her a better version of herself. This is not about changing the person, but giving her the tools to go after what she desires.

The wife was told by her mother on more than one occasion that she was stupid, worthless and that her mother wished she had never been born. Her only choice of work was to go to a trade school. Given the year she graduated, her only real choice was to become a hairdresser. It was not something she hated, but her husband also gave her the choice of being able to do more and spend more time with her children as they grew.

In fact, she started working with her husband on construction sites building houses as a family. It gave her more freedom to spend with her children, as well as spend every day with her husband. When she would ask can "I do this or do that," such as take ballet, he told her "you never have to ask. You can do what you want to do."

He gave her the power to try different things and be who she was, without judgement. It helped that they had the money for her to try new things, but all the same he told her they were equal that the money they made was hers to spend as she wished.

Now, she was also brought up in a poor family, so spending money was a difficult decision. She never spent money that was earmarked for bills, groceries, and necessary monthly expenses. She was responsible in the spending, but also given the chance to explore and do.

It made her heart open more for this husband. You may find that you are drawn to such a woman yourself. You also need to realize that while she is becoming a better version of herself because of you, she can also make you a better version of yourself. It is not about changing who you are inherently, but about taking what you are, loving who you are, and helping you be the best you can be even in the face of adversity.

The person who can allow this and accept such help in return is the person that can form a long term, lasting relationship with the right woman. It is also the person who will have the whole heart of the woman he loves.

Withholding Due to Fear

A lack of support and trust in a relationship can lead to the woman you are dating or married to, fearing to give her whole heart to you. There are subtle signs you need to look for if the woman fears giving her heart.

- She will withhold herself too.

- She will often go on trips without you for business or to visit family, and not call.

- She will test to see if she can live without you.

- She will test you in communication to be more open in conversation.

- She will become angry or distant if you answer wrong or continue to withhold.

- More fights will occur.

- She will start to ask where you see the relationship going.

These are fear tests that she is giving you. She is hoping that you will realize her fear and start to open up, start to pay attention, and show her through action not words, how much she means to you.

If she is not the right woman, then don't let her live in fear. If she is the woman you wish to gain her whole heart, recognize the fear, address it, and start changing how you communicate, offer her your trust, and support.

What do you do if a woman says she is moving out? Do you let her or do you ask her what is going on?

If you have established open communication, where she feels she can trust you, but is not receiving proper support or respect, she will tell you her fear. If you have done nothing to gain her trust, respect, support, or communication she will be evasive and tell you "it's just not working or it's me not you."

For the right woman, you will strive to correct yourself to make her more comfortable and recognize your fault and the fear of the relationship she is feeling. If you cannot give her that, then you need to allow the relationship to end, learn from it, and start looking for the woman who is right for you.

Are you Clinging

There are certain turn offs for a woman.

- She does not want to be your mother.

- She does not want to constantly clean up after you.

- She does not want to cook you every meal you eat.

- She wants you to make an effort.

- She does not want you to call 10 times a day.

- She wants you to respect what she says and remember what she says.

- If she tells you no, then it is no. Not maybe, not flirting, not suggestive.

- If she asks for your opinion or a decision on what you want to do—give her one.

- A woman wants a decisive man, who knows himself, and is not afraid to laugh at himself.

Above all she does not want a man who clings. She does not want someone who is obtuse to her feelings or the subtle information she is giving him. She wants someone who is willing to pay attention, to be supportive, who will try to gain her trust, and love her so she can open her heart to him.

CPSIA information can be obtained
at www.ICGtesting.com
Printed in the USA
BVHW040947030820
585324BV00015B/1172